the Naked Serviceman

by George M. Engel

"Serviceman-Service Center owner and User Group leader BARES HIS ALL - tales about the customers, Apple — the Mother Ship, the Vendors, User Group people and the Expo's. He's retired and doesn't give a damn."

A rambling, ribald tale of Macintosh passion and persistence.
                                                    - Guy Kawasaki

George is one of those regulars at Macworld Expo, and I always look forward to catching up with him. It's always a joy to be around his unique manner, sharp wit and genuine interest in Mac fellowship. George's hard work and dedication to his own local User Group is an ongoing inspiration to us all – and, he is never without a new Mac story. If you're lucky, you'll get one of his Mac horror stories.
                                                    - Fred Showker

ISBN 978-1-4303-1785-2

Foreward

Mice, icons, folders, double-click, click and drag, ram, and yes, even windows... they're all ubiquitous in today's society. Twenty-five years ago they had completely different meanings — or had never been heard of.

Over the past two decades, digital technology has changed nearly every facet of the way we work; the way we play; and above all, the way we think. Of course, those two wild and crazy Steves out in California played a big hand in the digitization of the world. From the Woz's first plywood box to Steve's glistening new, to-die-for tower, the Apple story is wrapped in a cultural aura like no other in history.

In the relentless swirl of technology, no other company has evoked such loyalty and devotion in its followers. Apple has spawned so many heros, legends and fanatics, it's clear the story isn't really about hardware or software. While the industry spins its promises of terabyte futures, the iLife and an iPod in every pot, the phenomenon is actually about people. The story is about a small company made much bigger than life by those millions who love the Mac. It's about people who would tattoo the OS 9 or 'Sad Mac' icon on their arm. Or people who paint their Volkswagens like an iMac. These are the people whose day starts with the latest Mac rumors and ends with an email tip from their favorite Mac discussion list.

Perhaps you've been one of those who idolizes either Steve. Or both. Maybe you've known a true Evangelist who stood in line for two hours with the hopes of seeing Guy — the first to plunk down money for the 'Netter's Dinner'; fought for a Newton Jean Jacket giveaway; or bookmarked Ilene's Party List. You could be one of those who enlisted in the Mac Marines to stand up and fight against the clones. Or, perhaps you anxiously await the latest edition of TidBITS or Cult of Mac. Maybe you actually know who Mac the Knife is, or attended the "Not the Mac the Knife Party". Maybe you own a tie-died "Raines" shirt, or a Mac wrist watch or a 'YUM' poster. If you are any of these, or happen to be a member of your local MUG (Mac User Group); or even if you just recently opened your first Apple box...

Your MAC-ification won't be complete until you've met George Engel.

From the early 1970s and his low serial number Apple II with 16k of RAM, to today's Mac powerhouse computers, George has been there, done that and managed to keep a good attitude about it. Well, let's just say an attitude. His depth of knowledge on the subject of Mac is rare. Aside from all the hype and celebrations, of which George has certainly been a part, he knows the innards from chip to chop. He knows the deep, dark secrets of the other side of the story. Yes folks, there is another side.

After IBM and medical service, George became enthralled with the personal computer and Apple. At age fifty he opened his area's first and only Apple Service Center. So in addition to being a Mac "geek" he quickly became enlightened to the inside workings of Apple — something few Mac loyalists ever witness. While most of us Mac users were happily becoming 'power users' from the original 128 to today's G5, George was sharing the experiences of those other Mac Users who weren't quite so happy. The Dealer pipeline and the black hole of Apple Service has its own stories to tell; and herein George clues you in.

George is one of those regulars at Macworld Expo, and I always look forward to catching up with him. It's always a joy to be around his unique manner, sharp wit and genuine interest in Mac fellowship. George's hard work and dedication to his own local User Group is an ongoing inspiration to us all — and, he is never without a new Mac story. If you're lucky, you'll get one of his Mac horror stories.

George says he's retired. Well, I'll believe that the day "PC's" run the Mac OS! Because I know that whatever is going on with the Mac world, George will be there.

And now ladies and gentlemen, the "Naked Serviceman" will share his journey with the rest of 'the rest of us' — adding yet another side to the continuing story of Apple and the phenomenon called Mac.

Fred Showker
Director: The User Group Network;
Editor/Publisher, the "MUG InfoManager",
President, The Appleseeds Foundation.

Dedication

▬ ▬ ▬ ▬ ▬ ▬ ▬

This book is dedicated to all those Apple II, Macintosh and PC Users out there who want to try and understand how this whole Apple phenomena started. Why are these Mac people so nuts when it comes to their computers? It's almost like a religion to them. How did it start? I try to pass on how it all felt to me and to those around me, and I was there on all sides of the triad; the User, the Seller and the Serviceman. This is all one man's opinion and how I perceived those times and people.

Thanks to all those 1,350 customers who have stood by me over the years. And to those three who walked away; Up Yours! It's nice to be your own boss... sometimes.

To my dearest 650 friends in the User Group, now down to just 200; I hope you're not offended by the contents in this book. No offense is meant. But the world is real.

For my children, all seven of them, who are going to think I'm one step closer to being committed after seeing the cover of this book, I love all of you and will miss you all dearly.

For my grand-children, who will think it's real cool, or RAD as I think they say today!

And a special thank you for my real close friends, Keith, who took all the pictures on the cover, and for Cynthia, who arranged the picture-taking and put the cover pictures together for the book. They're just as weird as I am and thought the whole idea was great fun. And especially for Cynthia, who saw a whole other side of me.

Lastly, this book is for my wife 'Arlene the Good, Arlene the Pure' who just smiled at me when I said I needed to take a picture of me naked at my Service Bench for the cover of this book. I DO love you too, dear, and YES, I did take my medicine. What a sport!

George M. Engel
Lakeland, FL 33809
© February, 2004

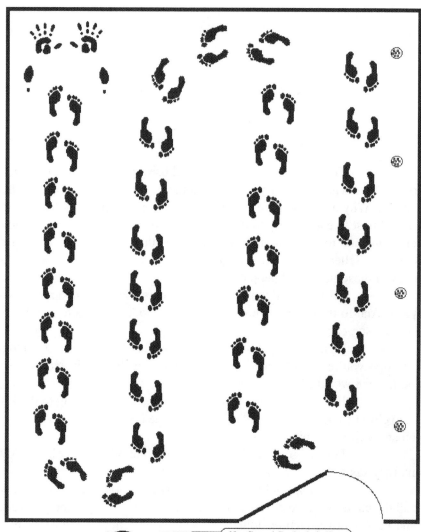

Table of Contents

CHAPTER 1

The Naked Serviceman

For me, this has been a long, long road. For you, this narrative is an 'outside the box' look at a Macintosh extrovert that's a people person, first and foremost. I'd like to give you an idea of what makes a Macintosh person the way they are. My early love with the conceptual computer, my torrid affair with Apple and the folks that love it, and the now-casual sniffing of the clothes after Apple comes home from a night out with the boys. Not that I don't trust Apple, but I don't sleep under the sheets with Apple anymore. I've been 'had' by Apple too many times in too many ways. I guess I now know what it's like to be a Microsoft user. Ouch!

This affair with Apple started in the late 1970s with my purchase of an early serial number Apple II with 16k of RAM and a cassette-loading tape machine. I still have the two cassette tapes that it came with. Through the '70's, 80's, 90's and into this new millennium, I've stayed loyal to the core. Lately, I've come to question our relationship. Like a marriage, you can give until it hurts. Then you start wondering why you bother anymore. This book is about the long road that I've taken and the people, computers and the phenomenon that is Macintosh. What makes people like us? What loyalty holds us here instead of to IBM, Dell or Gateway?

I'm not going to dazzle you with my technical expertise or name-dropping or how many diplomas I have on the wall. This is mostly a people book. People are what made Apple as big as it is. User Groups are composed of people. User Group people made Apple in the early days! People telling other people, and selling the conceptual ideas of original thought, of freedom of use. Of thinking 'out of the box.' That's what made Apple. Our present computer User Group uses the motto "people... helping people." That's what made Apple in the early days when they had little advertising. The little folks, like us, like you and me. That's what this book is about; my friends, my customers, my family, vendors, User Groups and Apple.

Hopefully, after they read this book, my friends and family will understand my passions and what makes me tick. Sometimes it's zany, and sometimes it can make you angry, but it's still a passion with me. My love of people and my life of servitude. I've been doing service for people since the early 1960's and haven't stopped since. I love the people contact and the mutual trust of relationships. Without that trust you have nothing. I've lost very few customers over those 50 years with people. People trust me. Therein lies my current problems with Apple. My customers trust me and my decisions for them, and I don't trust Apple anymore for doing the right thing for them. So follow along with me over my journeys and we'll take some side roads now and then. Don't mind me chatting a bit; that's what you do on long journeys.

Now why would any sane person... well, strike that... why would any person think of a title like "The Naked Serviceman?" Lots of reasons! One of which is that, for all my life I've been taught to believe that people look up to people that dress the part. Back in my very young days, when I had five children and was hired by IBM (THE IBM, mind you) right out of college for their (then) IBM 360 Mainframe Computer project, I had to buy the following: Dark suit, preferably black, black wing-tipped shoes, dark socks, preferably white shirts with appropriate ties. Talk about "Men In Black"; when that movie first came out, I thought it was about IBM Service Engineers. Their thought process was, and still is, Professional companies expect Professional Service Engineers to service their Professional equipment. Non-drinking, non-smoking, non foul-mouthed WASP's. And I went along with that... for awhile. With five little people running around with their mouths open, like birdies in a nest, you just have to put something in there. And remember, folks, in those days, working for IBM was awesome. If you put your body parts on the block for IBM as an employee, you had a job forever. Assuming of course, that you continued to play the role they expected you to. They pulled the strings, and you danced the way that Geppetto wanted you to. They were a fantastic company to work for, especially for the family. Christmas time came around and your children did NOT want for gifts at the annual IBM Christmas Party. But that's where my Dress For Success idealism came from.

When I changed my vocation from the Mainframe Computer world to the Medical X-Ray Service Industry, I maintained my Dress For Success theories that were now ingrained. Regardless of the job I went on, even X-Ray installations, I went to the job dressed properly, changed on the job into Levi's, did the dirty work, washed up at the end of the day, changed back into dress clothes and the customer saw me leave as a Service Engineer. That was important to me then. Along with a modicum of skill, lots of determination and long hours, the Dress For Success brought me advancement in many jobs within the X-Ray Industry. As Tri-State Supervisor and then Service Manager for New York, Connecticut and New Jersey, National Service Manager, and related positions opened up in different companies, I accepted positions and thought that Dressing For Success was important. Eventually, after over twenty years, I was exhausted from the rat race and opted out of the medical industry, back into the personal computer industry. Why? Because I went through two marriages giving of myself to my job and my people, as I saw it, and not enough to my family. After all those years, Dressing For Success didn't really work anymore. Sure, I advanced up the ladder, but at what cost? Two divorced marriages, many nights on the road away from home, nights literally falling asleep at my desk and awakening when my secretary opened the door the following morning and waking me up. Not watching my children growing up as I should have. Yep, there was a price to be paid. Success isn't cheap, folks. Somewhere along the way, I failed to look down and smell the roses. Thankfully, God saw fit to have my children realize that their Dad was a jerk back then and now has his act together again. Well, maybe...

I always loved computers, even back in the MITS Altair 8080 days. I bought my first Heathkit build-your-own computer, that uses toggle switches instead of a keyboard to key in data. Then I built a keyboard Heathkit computer, typing in hundreds and thousands of lines of code to make a program run. Even then, I was helping other build-your-own nuts to do what I was doing. Sharing typed in programs. That was REAL shareware, folks. That was my mental release in the evenings, away from the medical service industry calls of the daytime, and sometimes into the nights. Something was tugging at me, kind of a release.

At the age of fifty, I realized that I wasn't having fun anymore doing service calls. The medical industry wasn't 'people' anymore. It was a steel wall of corporations using people as a money generating stream. I wasn't dealing with people, what I enjoyed most.

My wife said it best. It's beating you down. You're looking for excuses not to go to work. This isn't a life. Even though I was making good money, 'Arlene the Good, Arlene the Pure' said she'd go to work to help us through the long haul of starting up my own business. Was she crazy? At my age? Start a business? Oh man, what a decision. But we went ahead and started the only other thing that I REALLY enjoyed and could succeed at. Servicing Apple computers. I couldn't wait to open up another Apple II or Mac 128k. I was dealing with people, REAL people who needed my help again. I could hold their hands, give them a hug when they needed it, call them at home or they could call me at home with questions. My wife relaxed again. She could now sleep at night. I was home, really back home. I was in love again, with people, my kind of people.

So here I am today, as a retiring Mac Service Technician, in my own little business, wanting to run around naked in front of a Service Bench. Why? I want to! I'd like to! As long as nobody came into the back of the shop, (and that brings up another point, later on in the book) that would be my rebellion after 35 years of Dressing For Success! My new philosophy… Dressing For Me! More on this thought later. What an idea for a Service Shop! Wow! Naked Service Techs. No customers would want to sit down in there. Free at last to do our work!

When the last of my second brood of two children left home, I went the whole next day inside the house Stark Naked, Nude! Because I COULD! I FINALLY could!

So, Dressing For Me, now comes without clothes, without baggage, and hopefully with a chuckle or two. Now that my son will be running the business, I only hope that my past customers won't figure out who's who in these chapters.

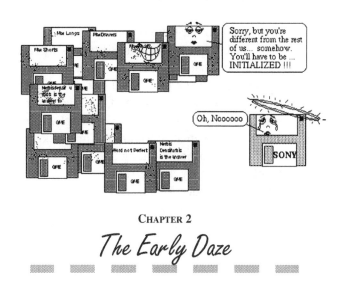

Chapter 2

The Early Daze

Now that I'm back in the old Mac days, I remember my first run-in with the Apple hierarchy. Here I am with my original Apple Mac 128k, doing repair jobs and soldering and unsoldering many circuit boards, making what we called 'FAT-MACs' out of 128k Logic Boards. It involved something like 537 individual solder/unsolder connections to many, many RAM chips and Multiplexer chips. Risky business, but I modified sixteen Mac 128k's into 512k FAT MAC conversions from 128k Macs before I blew one connection on the 17th Mac 128. Damn, all the profit from the other Macs just went out the window on buying new logic board. That was the end of my 128k to 512k Mac conversion business. 'Arlene the Good, Arlene the Pure' just looked at me and said 'How much did it cost?' in her demure Siamese-smile way.

During these Mac 128k conversions, I reverse-engineered some schematics (yeah, a degree here and there helped me to do that) to continue doing some repair jobs for customers. Apple never released schematics or component part descriptions of their computers. Never! Service Techs just had to do what they could, other than with Apple's Parts Replacement policies. In those days, there was a very high replacement problem with Apple's Power Supplies. The original power supplies had some under-rated parts, like the original Flyback Transformer, Damper Diode and High Voltage Capacitors. Three to five major parts failed consistently, and sometimes with major heat damage to the board. One time there was a charred hole right through the Power Supply Board, with a major crack in the Flyback Transformer and a blown Filter Capacitor with the top blown off. I wrote Apple and had a reply "What problem?" Sounds like the same thing today, right? President Clinton probably learned from Apple. Deny, deny, deny, right to the end. I was furious, our Apple User Group in Connecticut at the time had upwards of a 35% failure rate of power supplies/video boards on their new Mac 128 / Mac 512k's. I decided to protest this thing of ours. But how to do it... Here it comes, folks.

The first Mac Expo was held in Boston, as was all the early Mac Expo's at that time. I decided that I wanted to be taken seriously, so dressed accordingly. I wore my old IBM black pin-striped suit with the, yes, black wing-tipped oxfords and white button-down shirt and, yes, very serious tie. In my briefcase I had the very burned-out Mac 128 Power Supply/Video Board with a string around the edges which I then attached around my neck. On the bottom of the board was a copy of a letter to Apple stating all the persons which had failed power supplies (probably over thirty at that time), and a copy of my response from Apple's then – National Service Manager, which was "… what problem?" Another little sign in 150 point type, said ASK ME ABOUT IT! Well my friends, I was a little island of hope where many people said "add my name to that list." And I added their name to a clipboard which I carried. I made it a point to stop at my favorite Mac Magazines and to pay my respects to the Editors, for which I wrote many Game Reviews at the time. They applauded my guts for speaking out. Sort of like watching the Lions applaud the Gladiators as they were marched out into the arena. But at the time, I was angry and young, and full of vinegar. As I walked past the Apple booth, one gentleman came out and introduced himself and asked "What's the problem?" Immediately a small crowd started to gather around as I stated the problem and Apple's indifference to it. He then called out Apple's National Service Manager, who then proceeded to tell me that my facts were made up and untrue, and that Apple does NOT have a problem with those boards. At that time the crowd started to laugh at him and vocally started agree-ing with me, and what indeed was Apple going to do? He retreated and I was left to wander around again. I visited some of my Techie Booths, where Techies and Programmers abounded behind the tables. A couple of well known people, who will remain unknown due to their high visibility status today, gave me names, addresses and phone numbers of places where I could buy those parts that Apple used EXCLUSIVELY for the Power Supplies. Kind of like, passwords that you had to use on the phone when you called. Now I was in Mac Heaven, folks. The hell with Apple, I could now buy all the Flyback Transformers and components I needed. My search for the Holy Grail was concluded.

Oh yeah, by the way, I was also interviewed very near the Apple booth by a member of the Boston Globe for the local newspaper, who was there to cover the Expo. I told him exactly why I was protesting Apple's Service poli-cies at the time. About a 10 minute interview, while the Apple people watched, and the reporter took some pictures of me in front of the Apple booth. Ouch! (And the lions applauded, as they passed out the dinnerware.)

After parading past the Apple booth one more time and watch-ing Apple's National Accounts Manager picking up the phone, I walked back to my favorite Magazine's Editor to clue him in as to what I found out, as an aside. While I was there, two burly Security Guards approached me and with one hand on each arm, told me that I had to leave. No questions asked. In front of the

Editor, I asked why I had to leave. They pointed to my sign and said I was advertising illegally. I said I was conducting an interview. The Editor said I was doing a piece for "XYZ" magazine. The security people, chagrined, had to leave me alone. They walked back to the Apple booth and I saw a very frustrated National Accounts Manager coping with it. I made my point and the next day I returned to a very normal Expo attire and visited all my new-found friends who applauded my stand. I felt very proud of myself and humbled in that I got away with it. But I got all the parts that I needed for future repairs from all over the place. That was the start of my Mac Repair business (on the side, of course). Wait, wait, it's not over yet.

Many years later, maybe 5 years or so, I was a Service Manager for Computer Factory (out of business now) and attended some courses at the Apple training center for Service Managers, near Rochester, New York. There were about twenty people there, most of whom I knew, and it went very well. As we went for a break in the Lunch Room, I sat down to eat and who sat down next to me but the National Accounts Manager of that Expo long ago. That very same guy! As he sat, I turned my head the other way and tried to engage the guy next to me in some conversation. He then left, and I turned and found the Apple guy looking at me. I noticed he stopped drinking his coke and looked at me and said "don't I know you?" I said probably, I've been here many times and shook his hand and asked him what he did, etc. I just kept the conversation centered on HIS job, HIS career, etc., and not the back seat of my pants. I believe I made it through the day, but every time I passed him in the hall, he would kind of squint his eyes and rub his head, kind of. If he ever has a chance to read this book ...GOTCHA!

Even with all their problems, I loved their computers. It wasn't so much just the hardware, it was a mind set. It was a sense of freedom, it was like flying away from the humdrum PC kind of things. The KayPro PC is a case in point. You have to follow their command-set structured way of doing things, which in those days was exactly that. No Windows graphical interface, but a DOS text-based interface with the computer. It may have been great for a secretarial machine, but for a thinker, a graphic-based person couldn't do anything with it. So the Apple II, with it's doors opening wide into the games arena and graphics screens, held promises for me that the PC's couldn't match.

The PC people at one time were bean-counter types that were looking at spreadsheets and word processing and databases. Stodgy, narrow-focused, one way, safe thinking people. Apple people were fun types, creative, taking chances on software and hardware kind of people. My kind of people. Over the years, this analogy hasn't changed much. In the beginning, there was games, lots of games for the Apple. With the advent of the Lisa and the doomed Apple III, Apple and Steve Jobs kind of spurned games and advocated the 'business machine' concept. We just kind of scratched our heads and went on gaming anyway. When the Apple III and Lisa died (literally) away, we were feeling better about ourselves and our philosophy of gaming and having good times on our Apples. Unfortunately, I was servicing some of those same Apple III's and Lisa's on the bench and in the field. Not a good time technically, since I was having a bad time avoiding lying to my customers. Arlene the Good, Arlene the Pure, told me when we were married: 'I catch you lying and the marriage is over!' I take that literally. So I learned the vocabulary dance when it came to my customers, especially in the early days. I wouldn't lie, I just danced around the truth a lot. Lots of dancing going on with the Apple III's and the Lisa. I was a Dance Master. Almost in the Ninja Class! You had to be with those computers. Apple really screwed up. Today I call it as it is. I even tell some of my customers to avoid some of Apple's more trouble-prone computers and Operating Systems. And tell them why. But, I keep my customers! My end loyalty is with my customers. More on that later…

CHAPTER 3

The Early Characters and Software

The real cool stuff about the early Mac 128k computer is that you could have the System and the MacWrite application on one 400k floppy disk, and still have lots of room to save your text files on. The early one and two-page text files would only take up about two or three K of room. One of my craziest characters 'Ralph, the Mac Molester' bought his Mac 128k after trying it out for about two days, and told the salesman that he wanted three of those 400k floppies, because that should 'last him for a year or two.' Then he met me, the Mac program collector!

I gave Ralph his nickname because after I showed him ResEdit (a program to edit and make changes to files on the programmers' level), he had this crazy notion that he should be making changes to every program file he owns, including the System and Finder. His 'Dialog' boxes were never the same after that. Playboy Bunny pictures would pop up at strange and unexpected times and you just would not know what to expect. After replacing his System Folder for the umpteenth time, I tried to cure him of this self-destructive urge, but it never took hold. He still does weird things and pays the price. But at least now he backs up VERY regularly! He's also going to install OS X very soon. May God have mercy on his soul, for I know what's going to happen.

Another character is my very dear friend, who passed away a year ago. John was an Engineer's Engineer; a master at his trade. Not an enemy in the world. John would look at his desktop and keep it very neat. But inside the hard drives' icon, John always felt that he should organize and categorize everything so that he could find things at a moments notice. Sound familiar? Lots of people think like this, right?

As an aside, I've been down this road so many times myself, that I could see it coming. As the clubs' program Librarian in the older days, I was categorizing tens of thousands of programs, pictures and files in all kinds of categories. I had sub-categories within sub-categories within categories. Very detailed stuff. My library printout at one time was about 400 pages of items, about 80 items to a page, with an explanation of each item. Then, you'd always have a member or two ask for a printout of the club library. "What, are you nuts?" "You want me to print you out 400 pages on my Imagewriter printer?" And they'd look at you as if you had two heads. It just couldn't register on them what they were asking. This was obviously before external media or CD's, folks.

I appreciate what John wanted to do, but let him do whatever was best for him. People think differently, and not all people would file things in the same place. John would spend months categorizing things with different colored tabs on his disks, swapping files according to his new filing system. Then, one day, he'd come in with a new idea, using special boxes with organized tabs on them. Off he'd go again. He'd come in for coffee every morning and give us an update on his progress. With new media on the market, he'd change again to Zip disks, and then later on to CD's. Somewhere in the middle of all his transitions, he'd stop coming over to my house to see the latest stuff I'd be downloading for shareware and freeware, because I'd be so enthused with something that he'd want to take it home and try it out. Eventually, his 'pile to be sorted' was bigger than his 'things I'm currently working on' pile, and John told me he'd not be bringing Zips' over to my house anymore. We had a cup of coffee on that. My treat! I don't think John ever got 'even' with his piles of stuff before he passed on. But I sure gave him lots of stuff to work on into his retirement before he passed away! I really miss those morning cups of coffee...

Another of my characters is someone I'll just call 'Picky Nicky.' Graphics is like a strange world filled with elves and trolls and vampires to 'Nicky.' He just doesn't want to go there. That's not his world. His world is filled with numbers and words and forms and lines and boxes and... On the occasions when we would see his computer for a service call, everything would be lined up in millimeter precision, both vertically and horizontally, in alphabetically precise order, according to height. I think you get my drift. After we'd fix his machine, he'd get it back, with one folder 'slightly' misaligned! He'd never say a word about it, but I'd just KNOW!

Whenever I'd do a monitor or CPU house call for him, I'd have a couple of 6-32 screws in my pocket or a nut or two mixed in with my pocket change. After he'd be watching over my shoulder on the monitor take-apart, adjustments and put-together, I'd casually drop a 6-32 screw on the desk near where the monitor sat and drop a nut on the floor when he wasn't looking. He'd be asking me where the screw went, and I'd just say it wasn't really critical anyway. This went on for years and always drove him nuts. I passed that on to my son when he went up there once or twice and he continued the ritual. Once he came into my shop and saw my spare parts drawer that was just chock-full of screws, nuts and bolts of assorted sizes and it just made his eyes bug out. My son and I near wet our pants for days on that one! (That trip to the Sears Hardware section really paid for itself.)

Another loved character of mine is a dear friend, 'Dr. Bob.' In the earlier days of my business when I had to make it succeed alone, I was spending inordinate amounts of time at the shop. I'd arrive at around 9 or so and sometimes work on computers until six or seven, then refill maybe one or three dozen Laserwriter toner cartridges until two o'clock in the morning. On long nights like this, I'd usually get a phone call from a Doctor friend of mine who was just getting out of surgery at midnight or so. He'd drop over and plop down in a chair and we'd chat about Apple things or User Group things for awhile and then he'd go home. It gave both of us a chance to unwind from a long day. Many a night that would happen. Dr. Bob is a Urologist. A great guy to know... as a friend. Guys don't want to know him... professionally, if you get my drift. Guys are sensitive about things like that. Dr. Bob was one of the User Group's great Presidents.

In the dawning ages of Macintosh, you didn't have too many choices. It was either MacWrite or MacDraw. Pick one. Over time (a long time) we started to have choices. Over my period of Apple-dom, I believe I have used around 43 different word processors. A good third or so were in the Apple II platform, and there were many good ones, which some of you may remember.

On the Apple II side of things, I remember using Appleworks, PFS Write and my favorite, Bank Street Writer. What a great program that was. There were also some others that dropped by the wayside early on, like 'MultiScribe.' 'Beagle Brothers' also had great software for the Apple II, and it was very affordable. Then came the CPM cards and I graduated into the big time, using professional and expensive business word processing programs, like Magic Wand and WordStar. These programs had spell checking and thesaurus features that made writing a pleasure.

With the advent of the Macintosh came more word processors. MacWrite of course came with the Mac. The first Microsoft Word was a very fast word processor which did what it had to do without any frills. Microsoft File was a fantastic organizing tool and a primitive database. Cool and fast! Other word processors of the time eventually were Microsoft Works (competing with Appleworks/Clarisworks), Nisus Writer, FullWrite and my favorite word processors of the time, WriteNow and WordPerfect. WordPerfect was the DOS-users word processor of choice for office machines for the longest time. It would do everything! It was also big! WriteNow and it's further versions were elegantly small. WriteNow version 2 would only take about 200k of RAM to work, as an example of tight, as compared to MacWrite and Microsoft Word, which needed 512k. WriteNow was the fastest on the market, bar none. It also had the quickest spell checker out there at the time. I currently use Microsoft 5.1 because it's fast and not bloated with extra features which I don't need. Let me type fast and spell-check. No macros, no special formatting, no tables, just speed and size. KISS – Keep it simple, stupid.

For Spreadsheets, we kind of graduated from VisiCalc on the Apple II to bigger and better software on the Mac, like MS Multiplan in the earlier days to Wingz and Excel later on. Being a very graphic person, I loved graphic programs, with the earliest being MacPaint, followed by the fledgling Full Paint, SuperPaint and Canvas. They even had Desk Accessories as paint programs for the early Macs, like DeskPaint by Zedcor. It was an awesome time to be a Mac user. Today, 'Painter' reigns supreme as a pure Paint program. MacDraw copycats were Cricket Draw with lots of great goodies that they included. Then MacDraw II and MacWrite II and all those other "revision II's" followed by other companies. For doing my Newsletters, I still used PageMaker, the king of the hill. Quark was an upstart company which was always harder to deal with. They didn't stink, if you get my drift. But for my friends, I always suggested more inexpensive alternatives, like Publish-it! or Springboard Publisher, to name just a couple. But to this day, I still use PageMaker 7. It's just right for me. For others, Quark does what they want it to do. InDesign is Adobe's new Flagship standard-bearer and is a more complete program for the day-to-day producer than PageMaker, which is being left in the dust. Long live the king! Alas, long live the king.

Looking back at the cost of all this stuff that I used to install for customers, like the $1,200 SuperMac Graphic Video Cards and $6,600 Laserwriter II NTX from Apple that today we 'dumpster,-' kind of makes me feel funny. I just recently threw away over 15 graphic cards that combined would have cost almost $10,000 in those times. I almost felt like I would have wanted to frame them and put them on the wall, but no one would know what in the hell they were, except an antiquarian like myself. In some ways, I miss those old days, and the old names, like Radius, SuperMac, Moniterm and Sigma. Most are gone today, but the memories of those machines and times stay with me still. It was a good time to be alive in the industry.

Chapter 4

The Apple Dealers

From the Service Techie standpoint, I was there at the beginning of the Dealer Daze. "In the beginning, there was Apple... And it was good." Oh yeah, that was the heyday of the industry. High profit margins, excitement, everyone wanted one of those thingies to write letters to Aunt Martha. Forget that it was a high-tech $3,000.00 pencil that also needed a high-tech $850.00 impact printer to get that darn paper out the door. We NEED one! Oh yeah, it was nice being an Apple Dealer in those days. The margin was almost 35 percent or more. Lots of sales people, software support people, service technicians and delivery people. It was the golden days. One store in New York City had sales people by appointment. You couldn't get in the store proper without a sales person to go with you. "Sit right there, your sales person will be with you in just a little while." Oh, yeah, and the suckers sat. P.T. Barnum would have been proud. One gimmick after another started up and the people came and stood in line. You see, no one really knew what the game was about. It was a salesman's dream come true. Manna from Heaven. Corporations started hiring computer managers for the PC side of things. They already had mainframe computers where the software programmers reigned supreme in their own little fiefdoms and wore cloaks of gold. Now the 'ordinary' folks wanted their own little PC computers on their desks. We can't have THAT! Not in here. Come to us and we'll tell you what you can and can't have. WE have to do it for you. WE will hook it up and WE will load the software for you! And, meekly, the sheep complied. And it has been so forever since. Tradition is a very powerful thing. Apple people, on the other hand, were not so docile. We were 'empowered' with a creative tool. More than a tool! It was an extension of our frontal lobes that let us stretch as far as we wanted. We didn't need no stinkin' programmers or IT Managers to tell us what we could do. WE were EMPOWERED! We could network on our own. Any Mac person could. It was built-in. It was EASY! It was a Mac! It was Nirvana, a tool of the Gods, and it was ours. Listen to me, anybody. Let me share this with you. And the word spread. And a community was formed out of nothingness, like 'the Big Bang!'

In the beginning, someone would sneak their computer into the job, do their work in half the time and really look good, and be creative. Other people noticed, and started doing the same. Some businesses noticed and didn't like it, but with the increased output, looked the other way. In time, these little enclaves flourished. Advertising, and the creative marketing types, always found their own way to do things, out of the box, so to speak. When Apple released the Laserwriter, it was God's answer to save Apple from going out of business (along with VisiCalc). It was just the answer that they needed to stay in business. It was the lever that really got them in the business door. Everybody wanted to be a publisher! Paper was moving like never before. Dealer's couldn't move them fast enough. My first back injury was when I carried, physically, one of Apple's eighty-eight pound Laserwriter monsters across a parking lot, down a 50 foot hallway and up two flights of stairs in one lift. To this day I still get spasms now and then. But it did the job. Industries started up around it. Dealers started selling toner supplies and paper. Toner Cartridge refilling businesses started coming into vogue. Apple Laserwriters originally only had four font families, then finally released what they called 35 fonts, actually 35 faces. ADOBE did VERY well with their font sales. Those font faces were selling at hundreds of dollars per face, sometimes maybe three hundred dollars and up. Not that they weren't worth it, for businesses. In those days, they were.

Now we bring on the Clowns, uh, the Clones. As always, there was lots of money to be made. Innovators being what they are, saw that they could make a pile of money out of this, and started making cheap knock-offs of these ADOBE fonts, and started selling them with different names. Ouch. The courts made their decisions and they continued to proliferate. With font-making software on the market, there soon were hundreds, then thousands of fonts available to the industry. Today, there's tens of thousands of fonts, if not a hundred thousand fonts available. I must have close to five thousand fonts alone on my computer folders somewhere. Today a Font CD comes with over a thousand fonts for about twenty dollars. But I digress...

There was one business owner who sold Macs who 'specialized' in businesses, who sold the ADOBE typefaces to printers. He installed the typefaces, changed the names of the face, and walked out with the floppy disks from ADOBE in his hands. Yep, he charged the customer full ADOBE prices for the fonts. He then re-sold them again to another customer. When the customer had a font problem, he HAD to call the same dealer, not knowing what the problem was, and what the hell the font name was in the System folder. The Laserwriter printer didn't care, IT knew. That Dealer got away with that one for quite awhile. You see, folks, when everyone was ignorant, you could get away with that sort of thing. I had one customer call me for a second opinion. He was told that "the other dealer" gave him a $1,200 quote for a failed logic board. "What was my cost for replacing that Logic Board?" A few questions later and a quick site visit got me a customer for life and nearly the end of that Dealer in town. A new battery took care of the problem. Less than $70 for the total call. We didn't use a gun and a mask on our service calls. Granted, we weren't getting rich, but we were eventually getting all his customers. Enough about that guy! We might start talking lawyers here!

Apple's first printer was the Imagewriter. The original Imagewriter (it was an original Japanese printer, the 8510, I believe, that comes to mind) cost over $800 when Arlene the Good, Arlene the Pure bought it to accompany my Mac 128 purchase. It was an expensive printer that found a lovely place in our house. We used the heck out of it. I printed every font imaginable on it. I printed letters, newsletters, pictures and everything that could pass under the platen. It was like a message from God, saying, see, you can... I still have two in my shop today, gathering dust, with original print heads, that still work! Unbelievable, after twenty years. The Iron Horse.

One company even came out with something called the ThunderScan, which attached itself in place of the print head and actually SCANNED a picture or document, FROM the printer! It was a technological wonder that sold like wildfire. Everybody wanted one. Of course I bought one. I was a techie! I wanted it all.

My original newsletters used every font that was available. See, I CAN! It looked like crap, looking back on it today, but then... well, it was great. It was show-off stuff, I guess. It was wonderful, being alive. Every day was a new day of Mac adventure, new stuff coming out. They say that "in the valley of the blind, the one eyed man is king." Well, we had BOTH eyes. Imagine how we felt! And no one else could understand, if they didn't have a Mac! We knew, and wanted to tell everybody, how great it was to SEE. But, never having the vision, they couldn't comprehend! So we WERE a clique! And the Apple Dealers were happy to welcome us in with open arms. See our new printers, they'd say. Dozens of printers started appearing, in all shapes and sizes, for both Macs and the IBM PC. And we bought! Oh boy, did we buy!

The Epson MX-80 was probably the best of the lot in those days. A great printer, capable of good graphics, bit-mapped though they were. Especially when the font BOSTON and BOSTON II came out. I was really in Heaven then. My MX-80 printouts equaled or exceeded anything on the market, other than real typewriters or press copy. I was king! Or so I felt. Life was never going to be so good again. Until the Mac Expo in Boston came about. More about that in another chapter.

External Floppy Drives started coming out other than Apple's. Uh oh, someone is starting to encroach on Apple's turf here. I started buying stuff to feed my habit. Remember, folks, I was doing a newsletter on PageMaker 1 with two PageMaker disks and a single internal floppy drive on a Mac 512k Mac, which I personally hard wired from a Mac 128. NO HARD DRIVE. They didn't have one in those days. The System disk had to be constantly exchanged with the program disk to keep working, time and time again. My right arm is still stronger than my left, which I believe comes from all that disk swapping! So when Apple came out with their 400k external floppy drive, I just had to have one. My poor wife just continued to put up with me. You can see why I have to keep her now. So I now had two floppy drives. One for the System disk and one for my PageMaker disk. Wow! I called in my friends so they could see how easy this was. Later on in my development, I moved to a Mac Plus with a whopping 1 MEG of RAM and an 800K floppy drive. Then, of course, I had to have an 800k External floppy drive to go with it! Oh, the pain… and the excitement… and the ease of using PageMaker! And the original FileMaker (from Nashua) in those days was another exciting find. It's been exciting watching FileMaker go from programmer to programmer looking for a final home. And then to Apple, and to Claris, and to Apple, and to… Today, FileMaker stands on it's own, a cross-platform program that sets the standards, much as Excel does. But in the beginning, ahhhh, VisiCalc made the Dealers cash registers ring. Small businesses and corporations were beginning to see the great opportunities that were opening up with these personal computer thingies. Everyone wanted one and everyone wanted to be a consultant. It's like the PC world today. Go to a PC User Group meeting and it seems like every person there is a consultant. If you want an answer to a question, why, they'll just set up an appointment for you and give you that answer, for just $$$. Go to a Mac User Group meeting, and they'll follow you home, giving you answers and answers for which you've not even asked the questions yet.

For many things, Dealers found that the new Mac owners and their acolytes knew more than the Dealers themselves. Which started a different set of problems, so to speak. When these groups of users formed their User Groups, their opinions started getting a hold on people and people got smarter. They would ask questions of the sales people, which they sometimes couldn't answer. The Sales staff had to either learn the equipment or fake it. Some learned quite well, and prospered in the Mac fold. Others didn't, and kind of strayed into the PC side of things, where double-speak got them out of trouble almost all the time. It appears that you can BS a PC user most of the time, but a Mac user rarely.

The Dealers in those early days had a good profit margin and advertising money coming back from Apple, along with free software and all kinds of goodies. Gratuities from the PC companies for putting their PC's and their software right up front all made life good for the Dealers, because the PC's were going up against Apple. In time, the companies expected this, and considered it normal. Over the years, Apple started pulling in the rope, and tightened their belt while the PC companies didn't. Apple computers started being moved further into the back of the stores, or along the wall. To reach them, you had to pass the IBM's, the Compaq's, the H-P's, and the… whatevers'. You get the point. It's like trying to buy 'just' milk in the food stores. It's in the back of the store, where you have to pass by everything else, which is there to grab your attention. The attention span of the American shopper is pretty short, I guess. That's what all this market research is about. So Apple didn't play the game that everybody else played. They didn't want to pay the piper. You see, the PC companies were dealing with corporations all along and knew that kickbacks, sometimes in the name of discounts and freebies were the name of the game for sales to take place. Apple didn't play that game. They didn't have to. They were APPLE! The mindset starts! One of the ways that the Dealer offset costs in those days was to give away their services as a means of discount. NOW you start rubbing me the wrong way! Instead of a Sales - Service partnership, you now have a Sales - whore partnership. Buy my computer stuff and I'll lend you my service guy. Use him any way you want for an hour and then send him back to me, whipped and beaten. No way do I stand for that! Not for me, not for my service technicians. It was the beginning of the 'Us against Them' phase of my life with Computer Factory.

CHAPTER 5

Control — from whom?

Alright, who wants to be in charge here? And not a hand shows! Yep, sounds like a Computer User Group meeting alright. So the old guy who remembers the VIC-20 stands up and says, "Now in the old days, before there was dirt..." Now that's my cue! I remember my first Apple (post IBM 360 mainframe days) II computer. 16k RAM and a cassette reader. No floppies in those days. The first cassette I remember was of a square pixel guy walking up a pyramid and down the other side. Wow! The first Hi-Res color was of the San Francisco Bay, I think it was, by Bruce Tognazzini (hope I'm right there). Awesome thing in those days. Everything had to be loaded by cassette before running, and sometimes, in fact most times, the first load didn't work and you had to do it a second time. But, still better than my hand-built Heathkit computer that you had to switch the registers by hand to load the programs in. Man, the day wasn't long enough. I remember typing in a 1,000 line BASIC program, only to have the Heathkit quit at the 995th entry line. No saving possible there, folks, good-bye!

Then there was the time that Arlene the Good, Arlene the Pure stayed up until 2 in the morning typing in something for me on an Apple II CPM word processor (had to install a CPM card in the old Apple II for that) called Magic Wand, if memory serves me right, and I was going to just format it for her after she dragged herself to bed. Formatting only takes a couple of minutes. Whoops, I erased it some way or another. Damned CPM, it's like today's UNIX commands. I was NOT about to wake her up and ask her to re-type it! And it had to be done for the manager of my department. I typed it myself, all two fingers, until almost six in the morning. I didn't tell her about that fiasco until years later. Too embarrassed, I guess. First lesson in backing up, and I blew it, big time. That was after I told her about backing up. Now you know why I waited for years to tell her about it.

There was my Apple II, then the Apple II+, and then the Apple IIe, which was a god-send to me. I loved it. Apple User Groups started springing up all over the country. Everybody started writing programs for it and sharing them via their User Groups. At one point I had ten plug-in cards for those seven slots, of which two slots held all four of my 5-1/4 inch floppy drives. Lots of card-switching going on within my little Apple II's.

I also had a couple of monitors. The early monitors were black and white. I covered the screen of mine with green celophane and the other monitor with orange. Cool stuff. I was ahead of my time. Instead of spending big bucks for high-tech colored phosphor monitors, I was spending three dollars for low-tech patches for big-tech looking results. I passed that one on to the User Group people.

I had one of the first Mac 128k Macs in the Northeast. Someone at Harvard owed me a BIG favor, and I collected it by being one of the first in line for a Mac 128k on introduction day. Didn't know what in the hell I was going to use it for, but I was one of the first. No printer, but it was cool. After my first Mac 128 purchase, I waited for over a year to get my promised MacDraw from Apple, which never happened, by the way. That was the start of the Mac charisma. Apple II'ers and Mac fanatics started swearing at each other. Those were the good old days. And I had both. I was the Apple II software king in those days. But the Mac only had two programs for that first year, MacWrite and MacPaint! That was it! It was a wonder that the Mac's survived. Three miracles happened for Apple in those days. The Laserwriter, VisiCalc and Guy Kawasaki. The first two saved Apple, like an edict from God. The last saved Apple from themselves with their User Groups. Guy, as the Apple Evangelist, proved himself time and time again, smooching everybody into believing, believing, and believing that Apple was right around the corner into delivering the next manna from Heaven. Hold on, he'd say. Eventually, he delivered. One day, as an Apple President of the Group, I got a box in the mail. It contained a disk wallet from Guy Kawasaki, and Apple. When I opened it, I couldn't believe my eyes! It was loaded with all kinds of software! Remember now, folks, this was in the days that three programs constituted a full library! I saw about eight or nine full programs! Whoa, was I impressed! Notice all my exclamation points here, folks. I mean every single one of them. Phones were ringing all over the place. And not a one of them was copied to anybody! This was prime copyright software meant for demos. Not a User Group President I knew of copied any of that for anybody. Demos that blew the Groups mind on demo nights. Yep, Guy Kawasaki, the voice of the User Group little guys. The voice of the people. Am I impressed with Guy? You better believe it. I've bought most of his books, and had most of them with his signature in them. He's a person that you can respect. He'll keep his word. He believed that User Groups were the core of Apple sales in those days, and he was right. We talked, and talked, about Apple to anyone that would stop for a minute. We cajoled people into meetings. I remember when there was only my Mac 128 and about twelve Apple II guys in our group. Then there were two Macs, then there were four, etc. Over time, in our heyday, we had over 650 Mac members in our group. And this was a small town of only about 65,000 or so. Not bad for an Apple group.

Then something strange happened. A group called NAUGSAW started up. It was a National Apple User Group convention for Apple-only User Group Leaders around the country. Two or three User Group Leaders from each group were invited to attend. The host User Group assumed the cost of each NAUGSAW and hoped to recoup it's costs by charging a pittance from attendees and software vendors. I believe the first was in Albany, New York and it was absolutely great. It was around two or three days of multi-track sessions on just about anything. I remember we had one of the financial treasurers from Apple attending and offering advice on tax-exempt status for User Groups and such. Programmers on virus software were showing their wares and offering demos and review copies. The larger companies started showing up the following years. What a great time, what a great concept! Following years, NAUGSAW's were held in Toronto for the Canadian participation and in Minneapolis and other cities. Where they were to be held was a boon to the group holding it and also a burden. Ooops, now the politics started coming into it.

CONTROL! The MOTHER SHIP started seeing what was happening. The inevitable started coming apart and others, more into the politics, would have to follow the story from here. But, I attended the first NAUGSAW and the next to last, in Minneapolis. I couldn't attend the ones in California. Our User Group couldn't afford the costs involved. Much of the costs came out of the attendees pockets, as well as their time from work. But it was great, seeing all these people, these Mac Fanatics all, these Mac leaders in their communities. These were the people who tied the knots in their groups to make it happen. It was one of the most exciting times of my life. These were the REAL Mac Giants, those who 'made it happen' in the streets. And I was there! I loved it. I breathed it. The air of expectancy. And it was ours. We were making it happen. All the courses that we did ourselves. Passing on the torch of what we each did in our Groups to make it work for us. Many notes were exchanged and many lessons learned in those days.

Today, Apple calls it the Apple User Group University and holds it the day before the Mac Expo. I've been told there's still some excitement, but it's all formalized now. Ah well, maybe one of these days. I've seen too much politics from the Mother Ship and from some User Group Leaders at the Apple Expo meetings, and I'd rather stay away from that atmosphere, thank you. Our Group has stayed independent for 25 years this coming January, 2004. We'll knock products as we see fit. If it doesn't cut the mustard, we'll knock it, no matter if Apple makes it or not. Even as a Mac Service Center, we told the truth, come what may. A product may die an early death, but we had to live with that piece of crap as a Service Center if we recommended it, come what may, until the customer parted with it, or buried it. And if we suggested they buy that piece of crap, Oh the grievance that we suffered. We did definitely NOT need another Gaboon Viper (explained in a later chapter) out there! So we told the truth!

Few Cubes were sold in our area. Beautiful they may be, but ... not practical, and too expensive for the job they did. Apple made better values. Same with that 21st Century Mac. My God, almost $10,000 for a laptop. At that time, a marvel of a machine, but I foresaw another Lisa in the making, and said 'no buy.' Luckily, it didn't sell in this area. But the good ones sold like hotcakes, and some of the bad ones we're still living with. Sorry, Mother Ship, no strings on this puppet. We do what's right for the customer. Luckily, we didn't sell computers, we only serviced them. Luckily for us, that is, but for the poor Dealers, caught in between a rock and a hard place...

Dealer margins were getting tighter and tighter and with Apple computer prices dropping, the Dealer was getting squeezed. He was getting squeezed out of the Education markets by the Mother Ship itself, losing that revenue, but still having to do the warranty work, sometimes without payment. Apple cut the Education reps servicing the Institutions with face to face visits and they started to lose sales there as a result. I've seen the results of that mistake here at the local colleges. Nowadays, the sales margin isn't enough to keep the Dealers' lights on by itself, and Dealers have to have other sources of income to stay afloat, like peripheral sales, good service revenue, etc. Sometimes, I've seen Dealers lose good Service people and hire poorly trained and, in one case, have NO service staff at all, hiring some college kid when he was available to work on them. And they wonder why sales are dropping! I've seen some Dealers' Salesmen walk people away from the Macs over to the Compaq or H-P side because they were making SPIFFs, or cash rebates from the Compaq or H-P salesmen to sell their stuff. This was at an APPLE DEALER, folks! Before Circuit City, before CompUSA, and before SEARS. Today it's all too common. Maybe it's what Apple is about today, folks, and what it's been about all along. When Mother Apple is tightening her belt, guess what happens? When you starve with a Tiger, the Tiger starves last!

We all care, because we love the product, and we feel hurt and neglected because Mother ignores us, and we're her children. But the facts remain, children, and it hurts. MOTHER doesn't love you, MOTHER will not sleep with you. For MOTHER, you are a revenue source, plain and simple. MOTHER is a company, bent on survival. You are in the food chain. Duh! It's still the best computer platform out there, and we love it. Even knowing what I just said, and knowing that MOTHER APPLE wants me to part with my money for their next product, I still love her. But I know that MOTHER can be a bitch on wheels, so I proceed carefully. I shop very wisely. I converse, I touch, I read reviews, and I never, EVER buy any version 0 software from

Apple. The best of which was 7.5.5, 7.6.1, 8.1, 8.6, and 9.1. No matter what is said, at present I have over 225,000 files on my 3 big multi-GB hard drives and I'm sure that most all of them will only work on Classic Mode, so why would I run OS X just to be in Classic all the time? Not yet, thank you, I'll stay with my very reliable 9.1 for the present. It hasn't burped in five months of daily running. If I was buying my first Mac, then OS X would be my choice, of course. If I had few programs, I'd still do OS X (the present version, of course). In time, I'll do it. I do have an iMac next to my loaded G4/500 that I'm using. I play with OS X on the iMac, but do my work on my other Boss machine. That is, until MOTHER realizes what's happening. Maybe she'll make it worth my while somewhere along the line... Naaaaaaaahhhh, not in anyone's lifetime that's reading this book.

More on Mother in a later chapter...

Not tonight, I have a headache...

CHAPTER 6

On the Bench

▬▬▬ ▬▬▬ ▬▬▬ ▬▬▬ ▬▬▬ ▬▬▬ ▬▬▬

Cheap at half the price.

Our shop service rates are only $60 per hour on the bench. The big cities, like NYC and Boston, can charge around $125 to $135 an hour, bench time. Some places even charge a storage fee, per item! How can they get away with that? Good question, but, if you're the best or only show in town... We never raised our prices just because we could. We kept them lower and gave the customers more than what they expected. If I knew that the customer had children of a certain age, I'd load up their hard drive with learning games that were freeware or shareware that I had a library of for my customers. If their wife would like a game or two, I'd be happy to put one on for them also. Many of our women customers got hooked on the games I put on, like 'Snood,' 'Jewel Box,' or 'Candy Crisis,' to name just three out of the dozens of games I loaded on. I called them Eye Candy. One woman called me her 'Candy Man.' Some of those games were that addictive! Other customers wanted Startup Screens for their children, or pictures of their wives or children converted to Startup Screens or Desktop pictures for their Macs. All of this was part of our service package. Lots of this little stuff was done at no charge. This was what made us different. We'd personalize your computer, because every Mac was different, especially to it's user. People are different, why not show that difference in your computer as well? That was most of our customers. But then there were a few who were different kinds of customers.

A number of customers have demanded that we come to their house to fix their problems. We explain that we could do that, but it would not be economical for them to do it that way. We would have to pack up our portable hard drives, Firewire and Zip, with all their cables and power packs, etc. We would then have to stop the job that we're working on, and all that that entails, and then we might have to enable the answering machine, etc. All of that is time, not counting the ethicality (my word) of explaining to the current job owner why we're leaving his machine to do a customer call that we're putting in front of him. Then, there's travel time, both ways, and the setting up of our test equipment once we get there. At that point, we can either fix it via software, or bring it back to the shop. They STILL pay for the on-site visit either way, which is $60 travel each way ($120.00) and $60 for the service hour visit, or a total of $180.00 to tell this customer that it has to be fixed at the shop. Then if she wants it delivered to her house after it's fixed, well... you get the idea. So, we generally tell people to bring it in and we save them $120.00 right off the bat. If it's only an estimate, that's just $35 for a quick "no, we can't, because..." or a "sure, and it'll cost you just..." Most people realize the cost savings of bringing it in and will do so, especially when we go to their car in the parking lot for the ladies and the elderly to save them a trip. We just feel it's the right thing to do.

However, even then, a couple of the self-righteous customers still want to complain about our 'high' prices to come to their house. But if they bring it right in themselves, they want to wait while we fix it right then and there. Sorry about that, but first in line... doesn't appear to work for them. Their work just can't wait, it's SO important, can't we see that? Well, Ma'am, for just a $50.00 Emergency Fee, we'll apply half of that fee towards the customers' unit we're presently working on, and he just might agree to your stepping in line in front of him. If we call him and get him on the phone, would you agree to ask him that? Hmmmm?

They never do, of course, so we put them in the 'Emergency Queue' for only $10 extra. Right after this job, you're next, yes, Ma'am. No matter what it takes, uhuh uhuh. We have a number of customers that will ALWAYS have an emergency EVERY time that they bring it in. Watch out for the viper; you can hear it rustling in the bushes now, can't you? Any second now. Yes Ma'am, next in line, uhuh uhuh.

Then we have the security type of person who password-protects everything on his hard drive and doesn't want to let us service it unless he's there to watch us do everything. Maybe his experiences were horrendous with other service shops, but we can't service what we can't see. "But, I want to be there," just doesn't fly with me. It's $60 per hour to service without you, $90 per hour to service with you, and $120 per hour to explain what I'm doing with you over my shoulder. Typically, Servicemen do NOT like customers over their shoulder asking "why are you doing that?" all the time. It's very disconcerting. Sometimes you're just going on automatic and aren't thinking of why, it's just that natural.

I had one customer who said he worked for an Air Force Base (name withheld) and his Hard Drive had data on it, which I couldn't be allowed to see and needed his hard drive repaired. As it booted up, it required a password, which he didn't want to give me. I explained that if he didn't give it to me, I couldn't see the hard drive to repair it. That took a long time to explain to Mr. Security. I finally just replaced his System with a new one, moving over all his preference, including his weak hard drive security, which I could have worked around quite easily, but never told him that. Sometimes hard lessons are the ones you remember best.

The part of the Bench work which I personally like best is the hard drive data recovery work, where you come in on your white charger and shining armor and save the day from the wicked data dragon eater-upper. Recovering data from hard drives is a real specialty part of the business. Sometimes I can do it easily with my wrist snap-roll and bang, it starts again! Wow, but never in front of the customer. Other times, it's software intensive, like a one or two day job with the machine just spinning and purring in the background. Of course, we're working on other jobs at the time. The worst ones are where the platters within the hard drive won't spin at all. Almost always, that's a dead drive. But occasionally, I'm able to put on my latex surgical gloves and dissect the drive and go inside and get the platters to spin up. I only have to get them to spin once. Once they're spinning at speed, I can mostly get some data off of them. ONCE! Then it's dead. Once a cover comes off the hard drive itself, never, ever use it for data again. Consider it landfill at that point. I've been very successful in this part of the job. 'Good hands,' as it's called in the trade! That has always been a specialty of mine. That and fine soldering techniques, which are almost lost on the tech people of today. Most tech's are butchers when it comes to the finer points of soldering. Apple is correct on that point, at least. Don't trust your Dealers' Servicemen with major board component level repairs.

I've trained my son with soldering techniques by having him build me houses made out of paper clips soldered together. Where it gets dicey is when you build some two level houses with windows, doors and shutters. Try doing that without parts and pieces coming off. Also now try dropping it to make sure it stays together. Anyone can 'tack' solder two wires together. But to really stay together, they have to be 'sweated' together, both physically and electrically. Now imagine a two inch house, made of soldered-together paper clips, adding one piece without the other piece falling off from the iron. Yes, it does become a skill requiring steady hands and patience. It can only be taught by old-timers. Unfortunately, no one has the patience or time to teach those kinds of skills anymore.

I've been very successful and very fortunate in learning my skills, and I've noticed that the longer and harder I've worked at my tradecraft, the 'luckier' I've become. It's also nice when you really enjoy your craft and your customers. I've always felt like this, even when the customer you're talking to is not especially nice. Then you have to hold your tongue and just say a

"Yes Ma'am" or "Yes Sir, I understand" kind of thing. Luckily, I'll give those customers away to someone else and good riddance. Life is too short.

That reminds me of the early days on the bench, when I had a woman customer bring in a Mac Plus ($1,795 then price), a mouse that had it's mouse cord cut in half, and a keyboard with all kinds of crud so that a number of keys wouldn't depress. And the Mac wouldn't turn on. I asked her to fill out the service ticket and gently started to question her as she filled it out. It appears that she had a parrot, and this being winter, the parrot liked to sit on top of the Mac Plus to keep warm. For those of you who aren't familiar with the Mac Plus, it had no inherent built-in fan and used vents on the top where naturally rising hot air just vented on out over the power supplies high voltage circuitry through the hot air vents. Nice place for a cool parrot. Unfortunately for those parrot-sitting places, it appears that parrots have a short intestinal tract or something, and just poop about every twenty minutes or so. Just eat and poop, a regular fertilizer machine they have there.

First things, and easiest things first; the Mouse. Seems like the bird ate right through the Mouse cable. In those days, they didn't use solid wire, but something like a copper wrap kind of thing, and almost impossible to solder. Now, I'm a pro when it comes to soldering very tiny things, folks, but this was something that just wouldn't work at the time. So a new mouse was on the list.

Next came the keyboard. Removing the covers to get at the individual key switches showed me piles of parrot poop under and around half the switches in the keyboard. NO WAY was I about to clean each and every switch in there. So an approximate price was around 25-30 switches to be replaced at approximately $4.50 each switch, less labor cost, figuring 5-10 minutes per switch. Needless to say, a new Keyboard was also in order.

Saving the GREAT unknown for last, I un-torx'ed out the Apple Torx screws and removed the cover. Egads, there was parrot poop like small and large pyramids all over the place. Gently removing the bottom Logic Board, I saw Poop Pyramids on most every component that was under the vents. Huge mounds of Poop! Liquidy (my word) Poop that had hardened on top of, around and under the Mac's components, heating into a concrete-like substance. Eventually, all this liquidy poop shorted out some component parts and away went the Logic Board.

For conversation's sake, this Logic Board was a four-layer compressed sandwich type of Board with the power bus on one layer, etc. As a final sandwich, no soldering by a Dealer Tech could take place on the Board, as per Apple. Most Techies would have problems working with a soldering iron at that level. And, if Apple saw that you had touched a Board with an iron, no warranty would take place, even if it was new. "You touched it, you bought it" was Apple's motto to the Dealer. 'Replacement parts only' at that level. Apply just a tad too much heat, and you might just unsolder a connection on that innermost bus level part of the sandwich. Nothing you can do once that happens. The

Board is just tossed away. Total loss. These replacement boards were around $800 or more at the time using Apple's Exchange price. And, the old boards HAD to go back to Apple. Apple had them repaired and out they went to Dealers again, as replacement 'exchange' parts.

ATARI owners wanted the two Apple ROMs that were on these Logic Boards in chip sockets. To ensure that these ROM chips remained in these sockets on return to Apple, Apple would bill Dealers $500.00 PER ROM CHIP not returned! The gray market to ATARI owners ceased almost immediately.

Back to the parrot... So I added a Logic Board to her list of needed parts. Next in line was the vertical Power Supply/Video Board that supplied power to the Logic Board. Yep, you guessed it, blown capacitors and a cracked High Voltage Flyback Transformer coil and burned heat sinks, all covered with mini-mounds of... parrot poop. Add another Board to her list, about another $300.00 at the time. Looking further at the 800k floppy drive, I had to clean about an hour's worth of work there, IF I STARTED IT! Not just yet, thank you! All in all, that $1,795.00 Mac Plus would cost over $2,000.00 in parts to repair, less labor. I called her and told her that we had to talk. She drove down to see me, about a hour's drive. I showed her the estimated cost and she was floored. She asked what she should do and I told her... Dig two holes, one for the Mac and one for the Parrot. Kill the Parrot! I really was joking, mind you. Not knowing it was her love-child. She blew up at me and I never saw her again. My first lesson. Some people love their pets more than their Macs! How could that be? WOW! A $2,000 Parrot stand!

CHAPTER 7

Customers and Gaboon Vipers

As in any business, there are those customers that are like nails scratching on a blackboard when they call.. You pick up the phone and you hear the first word, "Hello?" Then you recognize the voice on the other end and know that you've been struck by fate. The Gaboon Viper hits again!

Many years ago, Johnny Carson had a skit about the Gaboon Viper. The shtick went something like this: Traveling in the jungles of Gaboon was very dangerous, especially when the Gaboon Viper was about. The Gaboon Viper would wait until you passed, then whammo, it'd sunk it's teeth into your ass and would NEVER let go; NEVER! The rest of your life, you had to live with this Gaboon Viper, hanging on your ass. Well, some of our customers are like that. We maintain our own Gaboon Viper list. Occasionally a new one goes up there, but it takes a lot to really qualify for that list. After 16 years of 'officially' doing business as a Certified Mac Repair Center, we have less than twenty-five Gaboon Vipers. That's out of over 1,250 customers in our Database. As you can see, it takes a lot of Viper to get there, and they NEVER leave! Never!

How does one qualify to be a Gaboon Viper. Well, let's see... Inability to think ahead or look backward might help; being the first one that the wolf pack would bring down could be an indicator; Darwin laughing at you helps; last being that both Will Rogers and Dale Carnegie are arguing as to which will be the first to punch you in the mouth. Last is the fingernail on the blackboard test. If you'd rather hear that than listen to that customer, well... you got it!

Here's a perfect example: We had a person call us on the phone and said he wanted to speed up his computer at a low cost. How much would it cost to do so? So we went into the pro's and con's of buying an add-in processor into his computer versus buying a new machine. Since money was the main question, cheap was the answer. So we gave him the stock answers. Increasing the RAM may be the cheapest, next is the Hard Drive size if you're doing major graphics, and last would be the processor itself, but processors are the costliest.

He then asked us "…why not just plug it into 220 volts! That'll make it faster at no cost!" ??? After gagging, we proceeded to tell him that just wouldn't work. He then called us a bunch of "… stupid assholes, of course that will work," and said we were "… just in this to make money." He then hung up. Which goes to prove, folks, don't argue with losers! They'll drag you down to their level and beat you with all their experience.

Another is the guy who just couldn't understand about Mac's and Virus effects. Finally we just said something like "… as long as you're on the phone with us, you're protected against that!" He was now satisfied!

Or the customer that says "I don't know if you remember me, but I brought my machine in there last year and I have the same problem again. Is that covered under your service warranty?" In our busy times we do about ten Macs a day. Duh! Our reply is "no sir, we can't warranty what you do with your software once you leave here, but if it's something we've done, you'll notice it the same day that you leave here, and it's correctable at that time."

Or the customer that swore we screwed his machine up and was going to sue, only to find out, after wasting our time for half an hour, that he had it done somewhere else. Oh yeah, some people don't have stress, because they're carriers!

One of my favorite problem bench jobs was an elegant Lady who complained that her Mac was just so slow! Over a period of time it had slowed up so much that it literally took about a minute between the mouse click and the action taking place on the screen. Now that's a long time. Usually that's a Browser problem with Netscape, Explorer or Eudora's cache folder filling up to the brim. Trying to open the Cache folder in her case took over an hour and was still clicking away. From my vast experience with Cache problems, I knew it was easier to just boot from another Drive, back up the whole thing, re-format her Drive, put a new System on it and drag her old folders back, less the cache Folders. Much faster!

As it turns out, it was almost an all-nighter. Her cache folder alone was almost 320 Meg and had over 9,500 cache files in it! No wonder she had a slow-down. I threw away all but around 40 or 50 files at random. Enough so I could show her what I meant by cache files. When this elegant Lady came back a few days later to pick up her Mac, I explained the problem and how it came about. I explained that the Browser keeps a record thumbprint of where you've been and the Browser Preferences determine how many thumbprints are in history, and how long they're kept there. So I decided to show her and her five foot-eleven, fourteen year old son what I mean. So I just popped a handful of the saved cached snapshots onto 'JPEG Viewer' and waited for them to flash on the screen. WHOA! What popped on the screen was NOT what I expected! Folks, I've been married before, but in all my forty years of married life... well, I was surprised! I've never moved so fast in my life as I did that day. I covered that screen to the best of my ability, and as fast as I could. My face was beet-red. I apologized profusely. This elegant Lady turned to her son, who lost about five inches of his height in four seconds, and said, "John (name changed to protect the guilty), we'll discuss this when we get home!" Three of us learned a lesson that day. She learned a lesson on child rearing, I learned a lesson on preparation before doing a demo, and poor "John" learned a lesson on covering his tracks and how to properly use a Web Browser and cover his butt, like "<erase now>?" "YEAH, damn YEAH!"

The Gaboon Viper struck him square in the ass. Imagine twenty years from now, every time he looks at his Mom, she'll remember how he embarrassed her and HE will be reminded of that for life. Or, maybe he'll have a heart-to-heart talk with his son on the facts of life, and relate how he got real stupid one day, and show him this snake on his ass, still hanging there. Now that's a REAL Gaboon Viper hit, folks! Yowza!

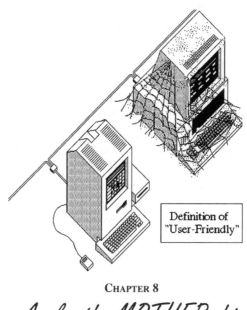

Definition of
"User-Friendly"

CHAPTER 8

Apple, the MOTHER ship

I remember back in the old Apple II days, and up to the Mac IIfx service days when Apple's Dealer Tech Support was working out of North Carolina, I believe. I knew most of the tech support people by name in those days. I dealt with them every other day or so. Dealer Technicians had to go to Apple Service Schools then, either there or in Massachusetts. Luckily, I went to both, many times. Laserwriter/Plus schools required you to totally gut that 88 pound monster, which worked like a dream machine, then put it back together. The instructors put lots of problem bugs and defective parts in it, which were typical of the bugs and bad parts you'd find on a service bench or in the field on a customers unit. And there were lots of things that could go wrong in there. You really had to understand the theory behind Laser printing and how to diagnose what went wrong from looking at the printed page. These were great courses by some great instructors. You left those schools knowing your product inside and out. I also tried cramming extra product courses into the mix, whenever I could, and the instructors were very helpful in making that happen. Those were great times and some very knowledgeable and helpful people. Those instructors just couldn't do enough for you. They also didn't cut you any slack on the final tests. You had to pass, or come back. Most all of the incoming students were new people trying to be technicians for the Apple Dealership that sent them. Since I was doing this from the 'old days,' I just needed my certifications and as many as I could get for my time there. I asked to work on two benches at the same time and was working on Laserwriters and Macintoshes together (usually two separate courses). Got them both. What the hell, I usually worked on two or three Macs at the same time when I was back at the shop. What's the problem? The instructor finally saw my point after he saw me work.

It was an expensive proposition to send a Technician to an Apple School. But you got back a technician who could do his job, the way that Apple wanted it done. Those kinds of schools were expensive to maintain and are no more. Even the old manuals are no more, for they were also expensive to mail and maintain. I had a one to two inch thick manual for every product in the Apple line, with product updates and revision packets of paper coming in every week or so. That meant going through each manual with update pages. In with the new, out with the old; ensuring that all my Techs were notified of all the updates.

Today's CD's are cleaner, cheaper to mail and even send over high-speed links. It's all done by computer today and more efficient to maintain. Apple has done many things right and has saved a lot of money in the field of training. Saved for Apple, not so much for the Dealer. Today's costs for being an Apple Dealer are still quite high. While you don't have to send your service-men out to Apple schools anymore in different states, you still have to pay Apple for the privilege of training your people by their CD methods and then to have them tested at an outside facility. They must pass! EVERY year! (Unless that has changed by the time you read this.)

There was a lot of paperwork involved in being an Apple Dealer. The paperwork involved in each service call requiring a part got to be hectic. Almost half of each of my day was involved in paperwork. Customers have no idea what's involved in ordering, changing a part and returning it to Apple for warranty. Every item must be correct in Apple's way or the reimburse-ment will be refused. Each part must be repackaged the proper way or ... refusal. And on and on. Your explanation had better be proper and written correctly, with purchase dates, serial numbers verified, part numbers correct and in the proper place or else. Even then, there might be delays in payment. I still had to follow up on missing payments to find out what the delays were.

Eventually, those payments were reduced by ten percent or so across the board every so often, then again, and again. It finally reached the point where on some items we never charged Apple for it at all, as the paper-work time would cost us more than the time for us to install a part. We'd lose money by putting in the paperwork. Apple wins, the customer wins, the Dealer loses. We kept this to ourselves, because it wasn't the customers worry. We just figured this as the cost of doing business with Apple.

For some models of computers, the costs of ownership and maintenance were quite low, but it was still a crapshoot for the consumer. Lightning storms without homeowners insurance or Surge protectors were not smart planning on the consumers part. Apple's AppleCare insurance plan was their answer for protection. It was costly but safe. For businesses or education institutions it was very smart planning, as this was a fixed cost per system that could be budgeted for. When you had a problem, call the Apple Serviceman and in we came. Part in, part out, have a nice day, good-bye. Apple took half of the AppleCare price, the Dealer got the other half. That was in the beginning. Then Apple took more and the Dealer got less. Eventually, the Dealer got very little (I don't know what the percentage is today) that made it hard for him to pay the Servicemen's salaries with the proceeds of service revenue from Apple.

Some Dealers were forced to cut corners with their servicemen, like laying some off, having them work less than 37 hours to avoid paying them medical benefits and the like. It started working against some Dealers and Apple started to feel it, unofficially. Our AppleCare Service Contracts went from a quarter million dollars in one year down to maybe ten thousand by the time the store folded. By the end, a service technician might make two or three dollars by writing up a contract that would take about twenty minutes to write. Remember, he also had to wait for payment back to him by Apple for that con-tract. Paid service was at $50 per hour back then. So it was costing me about $17 in labor to make $2 or $3 in profit. You can see where this was a loser from the get-go. We stopped selling these individual service contracts as losers from a service department standpoint. Besides, paid service was a heck of a lot more profitable, since we got paid from the customer right then and there, and didn't have to wait for Apple to get off their butts and pay us when they got good and ready. Besides, the longer they held onto your money, the longer time they got interest on it. Duh! You have to remember, this was the perspective that I saw it in at the time it happened.

I saw sales people taking customers right from the Apple dis-plays and moving them right into the PC displays where the computers them-selves were a little cheaper from the customers eyes, but as soon as you started adding on all the peripherals and extra service charges, the end cost was more. But, the salesman and the store made more profit as the profit margin on the PC stuff was higher. Apple's greed was hurting it. The bean counters and marketing weenies were loading up the old pistol to shoot themselves in their foot. We could see it from a service standpoint, but the sales end of the business wasn't in our domain, and we couldn't do a thing about it.

Today, that Mother Ship and their Dealer relations are quite strained. We were asked at one time to go on a service call by Apple Customer Service. We said that the call had nothing to do with the iMac in question, since we already had it in the shop at no charge to the customer. We ate the labor, since this was a real nice lady, and the problem was with AOL itself, and NOT hard-ware or Apple software. However, Apple insisted, so as a courtesy, we went, after being promised that Apple would reimburse us as a service call under warranty. The intermittent problem never showed up when we were there, so we did some preventive software work anyway. Billed Apple for software work and travel time, which was one hour labor and two hours travel time. A couple of days later, another call from Apple. Same customer and the problem returned when on AOL.

We told Apple what we did, and we were requested to return again and do a 'Clean Install.' But that's what we already did, TWO TIMES, we told them. Once in the shop and once on-site. No matter, again, they wanted, Apple will pay! On-site again we went, two hours of travel. This time, the Apple Dealer technician on the phone had to walk us through, line by line, of the litany of doing a 'Clean Install.' No matter that we were doing this since Mac Plus days and my old 5 Meg Mac Plus internal GCC Hard Drive. For God's sake, I bought one of the first Mac 128k computers on the East Coast. From the Harvard bookstore on opening day, around 8 am. Now I KNOW that mine was one of the first sold! However, not arguing the obvious, the Apple Tech knew we were street smart and followed the procedure set down by the Marketing Weenies. And along we went. Another three hours of labor, etc. AND another call a couple of days later with the same request for another 'clean install.' Again we said the problem was NOT with the iMac, but with AOL! Not acceptable, said Apple. One more trip. You'll be paid! You'll be paid! After all this hoo-hah was said and done, Apple paid us the grand sum of about $35.00 for 21 hours of labor/travel. It seems that, following procedure, re-imbursement was only paid on replacement of a defective part. No payments on software. Now we knew that! But, we said, we were told we going to be re-imbursed. No matter, have a nice day!

Just as an aside, if you've read the papers, you'll note that some Dealers have taken Apple to court on these matters and said that Apple owed them scads of money based on what Apple called 'procedural rejections,' or some such trivial nonsense. We're talking big bucks here. After these suits started, Apple's latest dealer 'agreements' started to say that you couldn't take them to court anymore without arbitration. And this agreement goes back forever, kind of thing. The Dealers that wouldn't sign it are no longer Dealers! Ouch! Have a nice day!

Where's that damn Gaboon Viper List! We have not done a warranty call from Apple since. In fact, we stopped doing ANY warranty work from that point on! Only paid service from that point on. They shot themselves in the foot with us! Now we have over 1,350 customers that we service. We tell them that it's paid service only. Most calls are software, and that isn't covered under Apple's warranty, so no matter.

While the Dealer and User Group relationships have built Apple into what she is, how can she turn it's back on us now, as if we don't exist? It's supposed to be a symbiotic relationship, but now it's like we're the poisoned Apple. Now I know how Snow White feels about Apples! Most User Group Leaders understand the feeling and the strained relationship. But it's the MOTHER SHIP! How can one turn on MOTHER? No matter what she does to us. So the User Groups go on, independently standing alone, and self sufficient (at least, the smart ones). Some real big User Groups have gone under, bankrupt. Smaller groups, without the big overhead, have survived, for a number of reasons. Less infighting, more cooperation, less money to diddle with, and a persons home phone number. Yeah, that helps.

At one special NAUGSAW (National Association of User Groups... etc.) meeting I attended, we were asked how Apple could help User Groups. Lots of suggestions were presented and very few, if any, were implemented. My suggestion was to have Apple include a CD or small pamphlet in every new boxed computer. That CD or pamphlet would have the name of every User Group in the country. Attached to each User Group would be a point persons name to contact with their phone number. This way, each new Mac buyer would have a built-in help line with someone to reach when they needed a lifesaver. It would also help the User Groups in attendance. That never happened, of course. I inquired, but the inquiry got lost. Their 'how can we help User Group...' memos just weren't taken seriously after that. Or they might say, we'd like to help you, but we don't have a budget for User Groups at this time. I've heard that one also. It always appeared to people 'in the know' that the pipeline appeared to be a one way street. For some at Apple, the altar of high-tech, that may have been as it should be. BUT... we were supporting Mother! They were providing us with cool new stuff. At a very nice cost with a high markup, but who's counting?

Yep, APPLE, she's a MOTHER alright. What was that second word? But we still love what Apple represents, her hardware, her software, her User Groups, her community. It's the beatings that hurt so much. More on the 'Mother' later on...

CHAPTER 9

Who is that masked man?

I had heard rumors from former Apple, and some present customers that they had their equipment serviced from Apple in their homes and were dissatisfied. Knowing that Apple doesn't have service people of their own, I was never able to pin down this rumor. Fortunately, I had AppleCare at the time, Apple's Service extended warranty, on our own computer equipment at home. One time, my wife's Hard Drive was beginning to fail. I tested it in the shop and was satisfied it was failing fast. So, I made believe that I was a customer (which I really was) and asked them for a problem case number. They wanted me to bring it in to the nearest dealer. I told them it was sixty miles away. After a little hemming and hawing, they agreed to have 'their' service person test it out and replace the defective part. I told them to make sure that the part was brought with them, as I couldn't take time away from work two days in a row. 'Yes, of course.'

My wife stayed home when they finally arrived and the service 'lady' would not admit that she worked for Apple itself. With a little coaxing, she told my wife that she worked for Kodak, Apple's servicing partner. She wasn't sure how to remove the G3 cover, so Arlene the Good, Arlene the Pure removed it for her. After trying to remove the floppy drive from the tray, my wife finally borrowed her screwdriver and said, "not the floppy, it's the hard drive over here" and proceeded to remove it for her. After replacing the hard drive, the 'Kodak Lady' wanted to format it for us. Arlene the Good said, "no thank you, I'll do it." "But…" "No thank you, just the same, and have a nice day." "Sign here, please."

Arlene just shook her head at me when I arrived home. After telling me what had happened, we proceeded to get her up and running, and we replaced all her software from her backup hard drive. Less than two weeks later,

Ralph, a close personal friend of mine, and an Airline Pilot, went through the same procedure with a "Kodak Lady" who proceeded to lose all his data when she tested his drive and accidentally formatted it. Then, a couple of days later she came back with the part and after two tries in formatting and initializing it, tried to install a clean system and lost it. So Ralph took over and let her go on her way to her next call. He called me immediately and said "You won't believe what just happened." He said, "The strangest repair person came into my house and screwed up my hard drive." Arlene asked him if it was the 'Kodak Lady." Now, Ralph was an original Mac 128k Mac fanatic who still has his original 400k floppies from his first Mac 128k machine. The Kodak Lady couldn't BS her way around Ralph. He can be kind of intimidating, especially when he's watching over your shoulder. That stuff doesn't bother me, I'd just make you hold my screwdrivers while you're watching. That way, if something went wrong, you're part of the failure.

Ah ha, so now I knew what some of my customers were going through. The only way to know is to play "let's pretend" as if we were children in the play house. "Let's make believe that you're the customer and I'm the repair person" kind of thing. Why couldn't Apple try this kind of thing in different areas to see what the level of repair was, which was happening on their behalf. People were thinking that Apple service staff were not trained in their own products.

Three months later, I was unfortunately able to follow the detective line a little deeper into Apple's own lair. The Belly of the Beast, so to speak. Near the end of the extended warranty's life, I noticed it was increasingly harder to turn on. Battery was okay, replacing the Power Supply didn't help the problem. Replacing the Logic Board by itself didn't help the problem. Replacing BOTH the power supply and logic board took care of the problem. However, that was with MY spare parts from our shop. A strange combination of BOTH parts would entail a call from me to Apple Customer Support, which I did and got my case number. Using my AppleCare number, I told them what the symptoms were (I couldn't say that I diddled inside the case, and voided the warranty!) and said that my Apple Service friend said that I should replace both parts. After wanting me to do a 'clean install' of software, I demurred, saying that I did that already, three times. "Well, let's go through it again," as if I was a novice. Remaining calm, I pretended to be doing it, closing my eyes and going through the steps with him, from memory, steps which I do every day on the bench with many machines. After he was satisfied, I said, "yep, looks normal." "Well, call if it stops working." Mentally I shut down, and sure enough, an hour later, mentally it fails to boot. Hello?

Calling again, they want me to take it in to the nearest service shop. Sixty miles away, I tell them. "Well, ahem, ahaw, we CAN have one of our service people bring the parts to your house?" I gently interrupted with "One of YOUR people? Apple has their own service people in the field now?" "Well, ahem, ahaw, cough, cough, well, one of our servicing partners will bring the parts down and install them for you" "Do you mean Kodak Service," I asked? "Well, cough, cough, actually, it WILL be Kodak Service, out of Syracuse, NY!" I told him of the problem that I and a close friend of mine had with Kodak, along with some of my other friends. I insisted that I send it back to Apple for repairs, but was told that it just wasn't done. I wasn't asking for an invitation to be seated at Steve Jobs dinner table here, I just wanted my computer to be serviced by capable hands, I insisted. After different levels of supervisors, I insisted on being transferred to Customer Relations. Again, going up through the channels, I reached close to the top and was told that there REALLY was no place to repair my computer at Apple. Apple Dealers and their associates did all their service. I was promised, from above, that their associate would take care of me in their best manner, immediately. Okay, I replied, I'd give it one last shot. Within the hour, I received a call asking about my problem. I told them the two parts I needed and was told they'd schedule me. I explained that Apple said it was to be expedited, based on my previous experiences with the outsource'd service company. Never saying that he was from Kodak, even when I asked him, he danced around that May Pole quite well. I really give him credit for his dancing abilities. The next day, I was told that the parts were in and would the following morning be okay? I set up the time and left work to be home when they got there. After calling them an hour later and being promised that they'd be just a little bit late, again, HE finally showed up. I had the old parts already packaged up, ready for him, when he showed up. He put the new parts in my G3 box, and I hooked everything up for him. 'Bong,' and I was happy. Sign here, please. Thank you, and on his way.

The average consumer would definitely NOT have the patience that I showed during these calls. I can definitely understand what the average customer would think on having service at that level. Definitely not up to our service shop standards, and sorely lacking in Apple's standard service fundamentals. I'm not sure who Apple uses for their out sourced warranty calls, or even if they DO have any outsource'ing of their warranty anymore. But they definitely had a problem and for sure lost some customers to the competition because of it. I know two customers they lost to Dell Computers due to poor warranty problem resolution, and we weren't involved in the service loop. However, it's just another way for Apple to make a buck by cutting out the Dealer chain and putting in an outside chain who'll do it cheaper for them (more on this later, as Apple is just starting to do the same thing now in Australia). Live and learn, guys.

It's just a shame that the Marketing/Service Bozo who came up with that idea to do an end-around the Servicing Dealers actually kept his job! Dealers spend scads of money to keep their people trained, only to have Apple go behind their back and do this kind of crap. Any wonder why Apple Dealers opt to sell other brands to implement their income? Apple can't be trusted to keep their word. With Apple as Mother, you have to keep one eye on the Cookie, and one eye on the Wooden Spoon, to make sure she's not going to beat you with it. But I love her still, as long as she's not in one of her moods. I now trust Apple as much as I trust Microsoft. To the customer, I say, always keep one hand on your wallet, especially when shaking hands with Apple and Microsoft. To be forewarned... etc., etc.

The latest way to make more of the money stick to the company coffers is to source out, or transfer some of your workload outside of the country where labor is cheaper. Microsoft and Dell have tried it with varying degrees of success. I have had customers complain that they have a distinct problem with the India dialect regarding service tech support. Dell's problems are all over the Internet with this one. Dell had to call back some Corporate Support lines back into this country because of it. One customer I read of, said he had 220 computers in his office system that will not be going to Dell because of it. This gentleman, who worked in IT Support, was treated like a new user and forced to answer insanely basic questions and resented it highly. So much so, that he will never support buying Dell again.

Now will Apple take this shift to transfer some of their support calls to other parts of the world with lower labor costs? That remains to be seen, but if they can make a buck out of doing it and still remain under the horizons and guns of the reporting press, I think it'll happen. For the techies amongst us, there's no problem. But for those new to the Mac and computing in general, the computer language is problem enough, without trying to learn a new language on the phone when you're in trouble.

Poor Apple! They get in so many embarrassing situations. And so often. Some of the things that they did I can't mention here for legal reasons. I can't get other people in the know in trouble. If I got caught with my pants down in as many situations as Apple did, I'd be paying alimony for the next 100 lifetimes. And they do it so stupidly! It's almost as if they know they're going to get caught, but they just can't help themselves. How about the iPod battery? Apple's answer was to 'just buy another iPod!' How dumb an answer is that? I guess you could try selling that to the average dumb consumer and see if that turkey will fly. It did with some, but some people fought back with reverse advertising in New York City and did it big time. Apple's immediate answer was to come up with a battery replacement program costing about $100 (not cheap) and saying that it was in the works for awhile and they just got to it. Yep, let's try flying this turkey to the press. Think they'll believe it? Yeah, right! This is not the first time they got caught and it won't be the last, if Apple history is our judge.

There is very few times in my knowledge of Apple brinkmanship where they have accepted blame or responsibility for any failure or problem in their equipment. From the iPods to the 'flaming laptop batteries' to the early power supply fiasco's of the first Mac's. Never did they accept blame, but pushed hard enough and they would extend the warranties or resolve the problem deficiencies. But, there had to be a stink in the press to make it happen! Why, oh why, couldn't they just do it without all the hoopla because they wanted to make it 'right' with their customers. The bigger Apple gets, the harder it is to do business with them. Their Customer Relations people are not the same courteous people that they used to be. Maybe they're just getting beaten down too much by problem calls by irate customers. At least that's what I'm hearing from the customer viewpoint.

One of my best friends had an eMac that failed two weeks out of warranty. The Dealership started the problem solving under warranty. After replacing almost everything in there, some things twice, the Dealer gave up. It's now outside of warranty. Hello! It took a long time for that unit to be replaced by Apple, with a lot of calls to Customer Relations. Lots of papers to sign, etc. Other customers had the same problems, right out of warranty. I've seen three eMacs fail just weeks out of warranty. Only one was okayed for replacement by Apple. We 'Dumpster'd' another one after the customer went with Dell in disappointment. Sometimes Apple should bite the bullet and say 'we'll take care of it the right way to keep you as a customer.' It takes a lot less money to keep a satisfied customer than it takes to find and buy another one. Plus, the bad publicity from the dissatisfied person is going to more than offset the expense of finding his replacement.

Some of these guys making decisions have got to realize that there's more to customer satisfaction than just taking their money at the cash register. We don't just get robbed in the alley with a guy in a mask. Sometimes the mask is on a corporate bean-counter.

Alllllll Rightttt !!! All you new recruits outtaa the shower. There's a slight discrepancy in the roster.

CHAPTER 10

The User Groups –

KAWASAKI: It just happened! As I like to say, I believe in God because there's no other explanation for Apple's continued survival. We didn't plan it that way, it just happened. Apple has thousands of user groups. Those are truly the evangelists. They're not paid. They're not employees. They tell people to use Macintosh solely for the other person's benefit. That is the difference between evangelism and sales. Sales is rooted in what's good for me. Evangelism is rooted in what's good for you.

How did these User Group things start? As I remember it, for me, it was a couple of people in the old days swapping their typed in Basic Programs in someone's basement and talking about what their problems were and ways around them. Soon, there were a couple of handfuls of us doing the same thing. Then, I was typing my little buns off and looking in the different computer magazines for more programs to type in. Lots of them were simple things, but some, like 'Santa Paravia' were real long ones. 'Santa Paravia' was a text-only role-playing game in which the family could participate. You eventually went from Peon to Duke, Princess, and the like. Arlene the Good and I would play this for weeks on end. It certainly made for 'a family that plays together, stays together' relationship. I would type in the program and she would de-bug my typing errors. And there were lots of syntax errors. Half the fun was in the de-bugging. Today it's all done for you, and it's all graphics. I believe part of the fun was in the mind doing the graphics. You had to imagine! Your mind imagines a lot better than many graphics designers can imagine for you.

So many evenings we spent copying peoples cassette tapes for the old Apple II, which were before Floppy drives. Users made the programs, folks. That was in the old days. Then came the Woz's Floppy Drive. The controller card for the Apple II let you have two Floppy Drives per card. Copy programs came out that let you copy programs from one drive to another. That was the start of the User Group days. Before you knew it, people were buying floppy disks two and three boxes of ten at a time. It wasn't long before a group of us were buying a case a month. Now that was program Heaven. Copy mania was setting in for many of us. Pirating copy programs started to make the rounds, as well as copyrighted software. People were copying software just for the sake of copying software. They had no clue as to what in the hell CPM was, but they just had to have it. CPM, in the old days, was like UNIX is today. You had to have a CPM card in one of your Apple II card slots to recognize the program. It had a higher level command structure that made their programs a little bit more difficult to move around in than the typical Apple II programs. Programs like 'Magic Wand' and 'WordStar' were awesome high-end CPM word processors and very expensive at the time. These were programs that businesses would use. Highly valued for the traders out there. These programs would almost set up a 'copy night' meeting of their own. Now I'm sure that the Radio Shack TRS-80 (Trash 80) User Groups had copy nights of their own also. I know they did, in fact, but I never attended one of their meetings. I did attend an Atari User Group meeting a number of times. That was the only computer I wanted to buy over my Apple. Their graphics were awesome and their 'Video Toast' program was so much better than anything that Apple could do. It was used in the commercial video world, it was that good. But, their User Groups never did take hold the way that Apple's did. But they still have some old time die-hard evangelists that are still around. I know one!

As soon as the Macintosh came out, the revolution really started. It probably took a little longer than that, for there were only two programs for that first year, MacPaint and MacWrite. All original owners were promised MacDraw, any day now. A year later it came out and I never received my copy from Apple. That's okay, I copied it at a swap group meeting and felt okay about it, as I should have received it anyway, free of charge.

In the early Apple days, I couldn't find anyone to share my Apple knowledge with, so I just evangelized to everyone. I printed out stuff by the caseload on my early Imagewriter I. I printed out my home inventory, shopping lists, phone lists, Christmas lists and anything else that I could, using all my fonts, and bold and underlining. God, it was awful, but at the time, I could! I was enjoying my newly found creativity. Arlene the Good, Arlene the Pure put up with all my craziness. I'll give you an example:

At about this time, I was involved with a User Group in Connecticut. My computer setup was in my bedroom on the second floor. To this day I'm paying the price for the following mistake: one of the woman members of the group came over with a problem that I had an answer to. I told her to come on upstairs to my computer and I'd copy a program for her onto her blank disk. Unfortunately, Arlene the Pure, Arlene the Good was in bed at the time. She heard us coming in to the bedroom and she ducked her head under the covers. My problem, to this day, is that I can't shut up and let a person leave. Like Mac people everywhere, we will follow you home helping you out all the way. So eventually, nature being the way it is, Arlene had to visit the little girls room and she couldn't pop out from under the covers. In those early days of our marriage, she wore what most ladies wear at this time of their marriage, which is either nothing or little lacy things. Eventually, my User Group lady friend left and the Lady Arlene made a beeline for the bathroom, mumbling all the way. Twenty-two years later and I still hear about it. I still apologize for my mistakes, and I should. However, in my early enthusiasm, I was an evangelist ALL the time, as you can see. Even in my bedroom!

As a Naked Aside, there's something that I just have to bring up at this time. I warned you at the beginning of this journey, I talk during my long walks. While I was in Connecticut, I was a National Service Manager for Raytheon Medical, where we pre-assembled X-Ray Systems for dealers across the country. We found lots of assembly errors which we fixed during pre-assembly and from which the manufacturing system was notified for correction. We also found lots of ways to quick test parts of the system, which I logged into my personal log book. Eventually, this log book was getting lots of tips in it. What a great idea for a newsletter! So I used my Apple II to make a newsletter for the Dealers out there. Printed on good paper with the Raytheon Medical letterhead it looked really good. One of my service people, Bob, traveled a lot for me across the country on Dealer-assisted calls. Being a nudist at the time, he would stay at Nudist Colonies for the evenings, or however long the service call would take. It was his call, stay where he liked. I put in for his expenses when he got back. I was constantly going up to Finance and explaining that he was saving us money by staying at the Bed and Breakfast Nudist Colonies. Finally, after months of hearing the bean-counters complaining that they have no place to 'expense' it, I went to the President's office and showed him the expense sheets in my VisiCalc Spreadsheet. We could either pay his $8.00 per night stay at present, or we could pay the Finance Departments suggested $69.00 a night Ramada or Holiday Inn prices. Which would the President suggest? With a grin, he said he'd handle it. (I just loved those VisiCalc spreadsheets). I never heard from the bean-counters again! So Bob was my original Naked Serviceman.

As an aside, I just returned from a long overdue January Florida vacation where I met Bob again after not seeing him for over twenty years. Yes, he still looked good, and yes again, Bob and his wife are still practicing nudists. We still laugh at those early years. He formed his own company and still services medical equipment, sometimes from his private plane. What a great success story for a man and his partner wife who loves people like I do. Maybe that's why I like people like that so much. But, back to the journey…

Why were some people so upset over the thought of a Serviceman being naked? Obviously, the bean-counters had objections. Maybe some people would also object if the same naked serviceman worked on their equipment. Maybe that thought stayed in my head over the years and led to this idea of mine about the Back Computer Service Bench. It was definitely not pursued in any of my newsletter articles back at that time to the dealers, even though they knew about it and thought it quite funny. We just kept it below the radar line for corporate. Well, back to the User Groups...

User Groups, User Groups, User Groups. All the time. Even when I moved to New Hampshire (working in Boston), and Rome, New York, it was User Group time. How my family put up with it, I cannot understand. In Rome, New York, there was no User Group, so I started one. There were two us, myself and an Air Force guy, Paul Turner. Rome, NY was home to a very large Air Force base at the time, It was a SAC B-52 base, where these big heavies flew right over my house, off one end of the runway. That's the price of freedom, my friends! After awhile, you didn't notice the windows vibrating and the glasses rattling. As the alerts sounded and the planes rumbled, you just increased the volume of your TV sets, then turned them down again. What noise, we'd ask our guests? You live with it and accommodate. Our new-found User Group in Rome eventually had over twenty-five addicts. At this same time, I joined an Apple II User Group in Utica, New York. Having both computers was an easy transition. My Apple II software library had over 80,000 programs of one kind or another, so I KNEW catalog programs! I had every catalog program known to mankind. My software library catalog reference book made me a natural as a librarian for the Apple II group. I was also the only Macintosh owner in that group, so took a lot of ribbing, much like the Apple/PC confrontations of today and yesterday. Eventually, the Apple II faded and the Macintosh platform came into it's own.

The early days of the Mac were kind of sparse regarding things to write about. Remember, there wasn't an Internet to speak of, considering the acoustic 300 baud phone things we had to deal with. So most software and software reviews we read about in magazines. Even that was scarce. Seeing as how I was doing software reviews for our local newsletter, I started branching out and writing reviews for National Mac magazines, including high scores that my wife and I were doing. At one point, I did over 50 reviews and was paid for it, believe it or not, as well as getting the software to review. Talk about being in hog heaven! My wife, Arlene the Good, made me stop putting her high scores in, as she held the high scores in three games for three months running. She kept getting phone calls from around the country wanting her current high scores. The last call was from Kansas City at three in the morning. After his reply of "Damn, well… thank you," my wife confronted me with the ultimate 'LOOK!' That was the end of that nonsense.

I continued writing my columns and my reviews for the newsletter and have been doing that monthly for about twenty years now. At one point, I was the only person writing and it was getting boring, as well as looking stupid for the Group. I started writing other columns, as well as my regular column, under different names. In one month's 32 page issue, I had articles by myself, Scoop Jackson, Phoebe Denquiste, Pierre Emile LeDieux, Ivar Thorenson, Harry Phontmangler, Titus LaFarge and Omar Reilly. For Phoebe I put on one of my wife's hats and wrote elegantly and eloquently on a theme close to a woman's heart, whatever it was at the time, using perfect English. For Pierre, I put on a lumberjack shirt, boots and drew a mustache on myself. Ivar's article was in technical computerese, as he was an assumed programmer working at the Air Force base nearby. Each of my assumed authors had a background which I assumed and played to the hilt. I even answered weird letters to the Editor, which I also made up and replied to, as the author.

At one meeting, I had one English teacher member from the User Group comment on my use of the English language. She pointed to Phoebe's columns as a place in which I could learn proper syntax. Trying to control myself from laughing out loud, I said "That's what makes our newsletter unique. The quantity and uniqueness of our varied members all giving us their own unique viewpoints on things from their own varied backgrounds." She finally agreed and backed off. I always wrote in character. Probably from my old college days, when I used to write term papers for people. $15 for a 'B' paper and $20 for an "A" paper; your choice of topics. Hey, in those days I had five kids to feed and a full-time job going, as well as full-time college. Lucky for me, my first wife and children put up with me. Those were trying times, folks.

Back to the User Group. I'd suggest to anyone putting out a User Group newsletter to fudge some names in there if no one else is writing. Make it appear that others are contributing also, even if they're not. You don't want it to look like it's a one-person show running the group, even if it is. Don't feel uncomfortable in making up a 'Letters to the Editor' column or anything else to stir up the honey pot. Be creative! Be original! Think of it as a fun trip to the amusement park. If it's fun for you as the Editor, it'll be fun for them as readers. To hell with the odd one or two readers who might be offended by a fun newsletter.

Speaking of fun, at one point in our history, we had a Local Area Network set up for the User Group. The Administrator set up an area for bawdy jokes and cartoons, with a password needed for those with a wicked sense of humor. I have to admit, I was an able and willing contributor to that area. (But then again, I was told that even Steve Wosniak had a website for jokes and bawdy humor at one time.) I love humor and am my own worst enemy, contributing many jokes on my own behalf. Making many mistakes and paying for them, my customers listen to me. It's in their own best interests. Best of all, I retell how stupid I was and what possibly could have gone through my head at the time. They love hearing about my misfortunes. Needless to say, the jokes part got real bawdy, with both men and women contributing, without getting personal to the contributors. I'd like to say it was all in good taste, but I'd be lying. Well, eventually it got out that an area of the web site was reserved for bawdiness and some members got real excited that it was there and wanted it removed post haste. Citing First Amendments and all wasn't the answer. Folks, for about two or three months of meeting nights it was real intense. I haven't seen people get so excited about such a trivial thing in my life. (Forget that at home they might have used implements ranging from buggy whips to feathers for personal use, but at a User Group meeting it's somehow different.) Now they didn't see anything bad, but they knew it was there, somewhere, and wanted it removed. It appeared to them that they were paying for it, somehow, and it offended them. So for you Board members out there, let that be a lesson to you. There are some places that you don't want to go to. That's one of them. At least not on a Server that belongs to the User Group. Ouch! What a lesson that was.

CHAPTER 11

Vendors

From both the Dealers and the User Groups side, you really have to treat the Vendors with dignity and respect. And, never, never, lie to them. Even if it hurts to say that you're wrong. Be honest and up front with them. In the end, you'll gain their respect for being honest. With our Mac User Group, I always let the vendors know how many people we'd have for them, if they were coming for a presentation. If we said 150 people would be there, we were always pretty much on the money. If it looked as if we were going to be short, I'd always start calling in favors from college friends and start passing out fliers to bring in the numbers that I said would be there.

The second thing is to muffle the outspoken ahead of time. Never, never embarrass the speaker so that they refuse to come back. Not everybody is a Terry White, from Adobe Corp. He's a polished presenter who plies his trade craft every day, and a User Group President to boot. You have to be tolerant of mistakes, both yours and the Speakers. Also send a letter to the Presenters' boss, letting them know what a great job they did, with a cc to the Presenter themselves. A little token of the Groups appreciation wouldn't hurt either.

Let me tell you a little story of what happened to me at one of the NAUGSAW meetings. I think it was in Minnesota. We flew out there and stayed at a local college or university for the week, courtesy of the local Apple User Group out there who set up the local quarters. The group hosting the NAUGSAW event would set up the itinerary and quarters for the attendees. ADOBE and Macsoft did their presentation and they were just great. Macsoft was smaller in those days and Al Schilling, the Product Manager came out and did the demos' for the company. After all the demos were done for the day, the big raffle started. Now there were about two hundred User Group Officers from around the country that showed up for the Leadership weekend at NAUGSAW, and everybody was there for the raffle. Now the prizes were fantastic. Up on the table were PageMaker, Illustrator, Photoshop, games galore and other prizes. Now comes the fun.

The first prize ticket was called. It was me! I won first prize! My CHOICE of whatever was up on the table. It was a Mac Owners Christmas dream come true. Everybody patting me on the back as I went up there. I looked at the table and made my selection. Macsoft's "DUKE NUKEM." You could have heard a pin drop. As I was walking back to my table, I kept hearing the mumbled words 'asshole,'... 'the asshole, ...'numb nuts.' The people that came to NAUGSAW with me couldn't believe that I did that. Why pick the $49.95 program when I could have selected the $600 PageMaker or the $500 Illustrator? Made no sense, to them. To me, it was perfectly logical. One, I already owned PageMaker, but the earlier version. Two, 'Duke Nukem' was in almost gold (shipping) for a real long time and was NOT out on the dealer shelves yet. So this was special. I was the first to see it. Not only was this special, but there was an Editor with it that you could use to make your own scenarios, and you could also use the PC worlds scenarios that they already made. Therefore, after you played the Duke Nukem game all the way through, you could either try making your own scenarios, or just download the thousands of ready-made scenarios that were out there on the Internet for the asking. I eventually had well over 4,000 scenarios for Duke Nukem. If I played just one per day, I could play that game for almost ELEVEN YEARS, without playing the same scenario twice. What a fantastic game!

The third reason was my feelings about it. The next winner picked up PageMaker and said 'the bidding starts NOW!' Before he even got back to his seat. Let me tell you, there was frantic money being held aloft. It finally went for around $350.00. People looked at me and whispered "asshole." Well, I didn't have the money, that was for sure. But, ADOBE and Macsoft saw some pretty greedy people around that day, and these were User Group Leaders from all over. They should have waited until the vendors left before doing something that made us all look that greedy. Al Schilling came over to me after the raffle and said "Why?" I told him my reasoning regarding the scenarios and the fact that I had the first Duke Nukem game that nobody else had, and also; I showed respect for the little vendor over Adobe. Folks, let me tell you, I looked REAL good that day.

Al told me that he had never felt so good in any of his presentations, that someone had chosen one of their products over the BIG ones. I made him FEEL GOOD. I told him that my unofficial moniker was now "that old asshole from New York." Well, that's what they were calling me! Al told me, anytime I wanted a product for review, all I had to do was call him, and it was mine! If he's reading this now, sorry for telling the story. But even to this day, we laugh about it at every Expo and if he's not there, I leave word that "The New

York Asshole" dropped by. Even when I call his office number every now and then, I ask for him and drop my name "The New York Asshole" and he answers with a laugh each and every time. His reputation was made that day when he got back to the office. David persevered over the Goliath Adobe. I guess that story got around. We had no problems in getting vendors at our User Group meetings in those days, especially after that story got around. Microsoft, CLARIS, Aladdin, EPSON, whoever we wanted and woo'd, we could get, if we woo'd enough. We promised, and we delivered, people for every presentation. We bought the product. It was a good time, for all of us, Vendor and User alike. We had mutual respect in those days.

ADOBE, the Queen of the software world, showed up at their presentations, well prepared, well stocked with goodies and were usually held over for at least an hour after the presentation was supposed to be done. Many, many questions were fielded and answered. Their people were always good presenters and dressed accordingly for the group. I'm always amazed at the preparation time that these Presenters go through to make sure that their demonstration goes according to plan. Even when a glitch occurs, they scoot right past it as if it was a planned event and a part of the demo. What polish! As you can see, I would NEVER embarrass myself or an ADOBE demonstrator by outwardly selling off a door prize that I had won while they were there. It would cheapen the product, the demonstrator, and myself. Show some dignity, folks, show them that the product is important to you, especially in front of a large group. But then again, maybe I'm old fashioned in a gimme', gimme' world. I hope not! Adobe software, and any software in fact, is NEVER swapped at any of our User Group meetings. It just isn't done!

Another thing I love about ADOBE, is that they were there from the very beginning of the Apple, Adobe and User Group triage. They knew the importance of a User Group relationship and how to nurture it. There always was, and still is, User Group Programs and Relationships with ADOBE. They know how important it is for the User Groups to get the word out to their troops. Most User Groups use PageMaker and/or InDesign for their Newsletters. Most User Group people praise Illustrator and Photoshop, the GODDESS of Image Editing software. It was NEVER an on again, off again thing with ADOBE, as it was with Apple. When Guy Kawasaki was there with Apple, it was as if the User Groups were important, they mattered. When he left, it fell apart, or at least that's the way it felt to the Groups out here in the rest of the country. It was never the same again. The reins were dropped for good.

With Adobe, guys like Rye Livingston and Terry White, their ace presenters, will come through for you every time, as long as you're honest with them. Adobe is far out in front of Apple when it comes to User Group loyalty. User Groups and customers TRUST Adobe! A bug in Adobe's software? Not usually, and if it should happen, they acknowledge it and keep you up to date on the fix. Apple will NEVER acknowledge a fault to be theirs and will go out of the way to spread the guilt on their vendors, if at all possible. Jeez, even Microsoft acknowledges their guilt, eventually, most of the time, or some of the time, if they're caught at it...

A lot of software companies have come and gone in this business. I've dealt with most of them in one fashion or another. I ordered some religious clip art from one company a long time ago when I was doing a church newsletter. It didn't work. After trying and failing to get resolution on the matter, I called T/Makers CEO, Heidi Roizen, and she personally resolved the problem and sent another free disk for my troubles. What a CEO! T/Maker was also home to WriteNow, one of the smallest and fastest word processors, if not the most elegant, to ever come to market. Heidi built that company up to a successful one, then sold WriteNow to WordStar in 1993 or thereabouts, keeping the rest of T/Maker very successful. The following year, T/Maker was sold. But what a company that was. Heidi went on to be a Vice President of Apple, and now is the Managing Director of Mobius, a Venture Capital firm. What a talented and beautiful Lady! She really knew how to keep the customers happy.

Another great company for User Groups was Casady and Greene. They used to send a box of software to each and every User Group across the country for distribution and/or raffles for every Christmas. New software coming out? Want to do a review for us, George? Okey-Dokey. Around 1996 they rented a ship to take their valued User Group clients and customers around Boston Harbor. We partied until the early morning, it seemed like. Food, dancing and a great time. Nobody in any group that I knew of copied any of their software. They had REAL loyal customers and great software. Apple hired Casady and Greene's best software engineers and made iTunes out of SoundJam, which I still use today. A really great music playing program! Ever since that engineer brain-drain, the company downward-spiraled and just recently closed their doors.

One of my favorite fun-based companies was Berkeley Systems, makers of the 'Screen Savers' we all loved. I was a long-time beta tester for the company and I loved it. I just couldn't wait for the next themed screen saver. Screen savers weren't really needed during the late 90's, since CRT's were advanced enough that phosphor burn wasn't a problem anymore. Don't tell that to the people who loved the software! We just couldn't get enough of it. Beta-testing wasn't easy work though. Problems that could crash your system had to be reported promptly. The software had to be tested under all your programs, looking for conflicts. Once this was finalized and 'golden,' you got a free copy of the software. However, if you consider all the time it took, sometimes having to reinstall your System and some programs, it would have been cheaper to just wait and buy the program. But it wouldn't have put you on the 'inside.' At the Macworld Expo's at Bayside in Boston, their booths were the talk of the show. Every year! They had great extroverted people manning their booths. I really miss their talent and their chutzpah.

But one of the earliest, and most beloved of all, was the Apple II's 'Beagle Brothers' company of fun-loving weirdos. Their programs were available through magazines, or you could type them in, or you could buy floppies with the programs already typed in. They were really inexpensive. They were so inexpensive that users wouldn't give copies out to other people. 'Buy them' we'd say! We were loyal to their company. They came out with real innovative stuff. Toward the end of their reign, they were so loyal to their users that it killed them. When they should have been transitioning to the new Macintosh platform, they listened to their user base and kept their programmers and support lines dedicated to the Apple II. That eventually was their downfall. They couldn't make the transition in time enough to financially cover their staff. What a shame. It was a very beloved company and sorely missed by their users. I never copied any of my Beagle stuff for other people's use. I loved that company too much.

Another two of my favorites were Claris and FileMaker. I still have the original spiral-bound, dealers 'FileMaker' manual from Nashoba Systems and Forethought, Inc., one of the original owners of 'FileMaker' before they were bought out. I bought that program in the early days and loved it much better than Microsoft's 'File.' I've updated it many times since.

I still have many of my early 400k disks, like 'File,' 'MS's Multiplan,' Paladin's 'Crunch,' PageMaker version 1 and 2' 400k and 800k floppy disk sets, and Photoshop 1. Oh yeah, those were the hey-days when you had to consistently shift between the 'Startup Disk (System software)' and the 'Program Disk' constantly in PageMaker. Oh my aching arms. When Apple came out with the external 400k Disk Drive, it was heaven! You could continue your work without interruption. At the time, I was doing flyers and newsletters, and everything that I could imagine (all after my regular work day, or course). No one could really make money on the Mac at the time, especially with Imagewriter dot-matrix printout.

Apple just couldn't break into the business world at the time. Two things changed that! VisiCalc for the Apple II in 1979, and the Laserwriter in late 1985 for the Macintosh. VisiCalc was the first spreadsheet, EVER! It literally gave Apple entrance into the business world in 1979, giving us the 'what if' instant answers to the financial bean-counters. Apple could have bought VisiCalc for one million dollars then and owned it. They turned it down! Bill Gates must have smiled at that one! Unfortunately for Dan Bricklin, one of the authors of VisiCalc, he never copyrighted the program or the concept, and Microsoft's EXCEL was born! (You can visit his web site to find out why not. It's at www.bricklin.com.) Why not, Apple didn't want it. Hey, don't feel bad about it. H-P turned down the purchase of Apple. So did Atari. It was rumored that even Commodore turned down Steve Job's offer for $100,000 for Apple. Hey, IBM turned down a cheap offer for a copying machine startup company of a few people. That company went on to become Xerox!

While Apple's original printer, the Imagewriter, printed very good at 144 dots per inch, there weren't many font faces originally. Please excuse my terminology of fonts, font faces and font families. I'm not trying to be a snob here. I love fonts too much to do that to you. There are loads of books on fonts, font foundries and the technologies that made printing possible. Apple gave you some basic fonts which were called bit-mapped fonts. The original Macintosh screen was 72 dot pixels per inch and the original Imagewriter was twice that at 144 dots per inch. What a great match. What you could see, you could print. It was lovingly called WYSIWYG, or, What You See Is What You Get. The original Imagewriter fonts were called 'city fonts.' The font names were called Athens, Venice, Los Angeles, New York, Monaco, London, San Francisco, Venice, Geneva and the pictograph fonts Cairo and Mobile. All but Venice were designed by Susan Kare of Apple. Bill Atkinson of HyperCard fame did the Venice font. Later on, font designers came out with their own, especially my beloved Boston II for the Imagewriter. Some were freeware, and some were shareware for a few bucks. The end-users piled on and it was great. Soon, there were many hundreds of fonts out there and the font conflicts started. Apple eventually had to clean house with their font naming and numbering system. But still, bit-mapped fonts weren't of any commercial business use until the Postscript Laserwriter and the Macintosh saved Apple's butt.

The Laserwriter and Macintosh combination were an instant hit. It made everyone (who could afford the $6,000+ Laserwriter and $2,000+ Macintosh) into an instant desktop designer. Newsletters and print copy were everywhere. Suddenly I was putting out a professional (at the time) newsletter for User Groups. PageMaker came into it's own right there! Big time! I still have the original 400k single-sided floppy disk set of two floppies. Since the original Laserwriter only had four font families (I think 12 or 13 font faces in all, counting Bold, Italic and Underline), Adobe came out with font faces which you could purchase at a goodly sum. REAL goodly, like $150 - $300 each. But that was the price then. Printer shops were paying much more than that for their professional typeset fonts. Eventually Apple came out with the Laserwriter Plus, which had 45 font (faces) and a better font downloading capability, which allowed the user to download Adobe-purchased fonts into the Laserwriter for that session. The font race was on.

One unusual company which I fell in love with was Emerald Software's 'Smart Art,' which actually used the Laserwriter as a slaved postscript processor and used the results. It actually sent the task to the Laserwriter and then downloaded it back into the Mac for display. It was mostly text effects, if I remember right. Awesome, time-consuming and very creative at the time. I think Adobe bought them out and it was never heard from again.

For every Laserwriter that was sold, Apple had to pay their stipend to Adobe for the use of the Postscript logic board technology. It was rumored to be around $500 per unit. Eventually, Apple tried to re-negotiate that price. Since Adobe was in the catbird seat, they didn't have to negotiate. It was a real money-generating machine. Nothing in, money out. Why negotiate? Apple, true to style, out-engineered Adobe by coming out with their own font, called TrueType. Where a Postscript font is composed of both a bitmap and a printer font, a TrueType font has only one, bypassing the printer font entirely. Using a Quickdraw technology that used the Laserwriter and came out with fonts that looked pretty darn good as compared to Postscript fonts, they had a winner on their hands. Even more so when Microsoft backed them and implemented the technology in their own software line. Ouch! Apple left the TrueType font architecture open also. Everybody started making TrueType fonts now.

Back to the font race. I believe that a court case ruled against Adobe and left the fonts open for everybody to modify and make their own names, even sound-alike names and get away with it. Fonts proliferated and font company providers sprung up like weeds, with prices dropping down to maybe $10 a CD with hundreds of fonts per CD. What used to be a postscript-only Adobe font now had dozens of look-alike, sound-alike TrueType fonts for ten bucks a CD. For purists like I and many other professionals, postscript is still the ONLY answer for professional output. TrueType looks good on newsletters, but for real output, you can't beat Adobe, or ITC, etc., postscript. So when you see these $10 font CD's, don't get confused and think Adobe's ripping you off. It's the other way around. Adobe, ITC and other print foundries (an old world place where type faces used to be carved out of wood and metal, etc.) have people laboriously making new fonts to become tomorrow's standards. This takes an inordinate amount of time and patience to be perfect in every way. Then somebody rips them off with a five-dollar knockoff in a TrueType look alike. But, printers and designers recognize the difference and wouldn't be caught using TrueType for professional work. Now you know the difference! I'm a postscript man, and an Adobe rooter, mainly for all their years of hard devoted work towards the success of User Groups. I will always wish them well and never speak ill of them nor do them wrong.

In the Printer world, I will always side with Epson, who has stood by Apple in thick and thin. H-P, on the other hand, decided to drop out with Apple in Apple's darkest years. Epson stood in there. That's what loyalty is all about. Maybe Epson knew more than H-P did. H-P was thinking short-term and Epson was in for the long haul, doing their R&D for the photographic journey ahead. It's hard to stay up to date in the printer world today, though. It changes so rapidly, partly due to the refillable ink cartridge vendors. Every time that the printer vendors design a new printer, they design a new print cartridge for it, to keep one step ahead of the refillable cartridge guys. Assuming six months to a year head start lead time, by the time you buy your next printer, it's already out of date. Epson has a little solid-state chip on the back of every ink cartridge that measures each time a page is printed. That way you can take out a cartridge and put it in another printer of the same model and that printer knows how much ink is left, approximately. I don't believe in refillable Inkjet cartridges, period. I have seen the result of too many Epson printers that had to be thrown away for that reason. Epson print heads are now down to 1.5 picoliter droplets, for crying out loud. That's putting a lot of trust into an ink manufacturer to come up with a solution that'll work at that level, reliably. We have found that a customer may get away with refillable cartridges for maybe 2-3 times. After that, things go south in a hurry. However, with the price of printers dropping as quick as they are, and the cost of a new cartridge, it's almost at the point of becoming a consumable market. Just throw it away and buy a new printer. It comes WITH a cartridge and a one year warranty.

Software   Support?

CHAPTER 12

The Users

When I bought my first Heathkit computer kit, I was really enthused with the adventure of it all. All those parts and thingies looked great. The possibilities of it all. However, the realities of toggling in the bits, literally bits, of information with switches, soon became tiresome. The next computer kit, with a real keyboard, now showed promise. Why, you can actually type in your own programs, like that 1,000 word program that we copied from the computer magazine and then proceeded to de-bug, line by line, editing out your typos. Even my wife enjoyed it, kind of. She started to get pretty good at it, after awhile. But she didn't get the same enjoyment out of it that I did, I guess, because she usually feel asleep around two-o'clock in the a.m. Sheesh!

Reading the magazines was a great thing for me at that time, because I was really interested in the field. I saw that a couple of guys were selling this computer called the Apple in a kit form. Paying it no mind, other than remembering it, I later saw it called the Apple II, selling for under $999. Color! Built-in keyboard! I knew then that I had to have one. I bought it, along with an R-F modulator that you could use with your TV set. It worked, first time. I was in love; again. No matter that you had to load your programs in via a cassette tape reader. It was great. I still have my first two Apple II cassette tapes that came with it! Two programs each tape, one on each side. Sometimes it took a number of times to load properly, but that wasn't Apple's fault, it was the Reader. Soon, I met others like myself and we started meeting in each other's house. Then, there were just too many of us to do that and we started looking for other places to meet. Darn, we were actually starting to get organized. The

Dealer offered his place after hours, since he was an avid Apple User also. "Apple ONLY" Dealers were the thing in those days. Many a night was spent typing in your own programs on cassette and swapping tapes. Why not? They were yours, and those that you had re-typed in from magazines, which were plentiful in those days. Then came the wonderful 5-1/4 floppy drives from Apple and the floppy disks which let you put all kinds of information on them. And the start of my servicing Apple II's out of my basement. Eventually, I had more software than anybody I knew, or even heard of, and I knew people all over the state, visiting Apple User Groups all over Connecticut and New York. Boy, did I know User Groups and Apple II's! I lived for the stuff. At one time, I had my computer setup in my bedroom and had a lady friend person come over in the morning to share some stuff we were doing, not even thinking that my wife was still in bed and had to get up and make a bathroom call. I just got so involved in what I was doing, I never stopped to consider anything else. How dumb I was. But that's the problem of being so single-focused. I guess I was always very focused on what I was doing. Some say I'm self-centered. I'm not. I think it's just being so focused on what you're doing and not seeing anything else around you. I'm sure that's what I was doing in those days. But the Lady Arlene stayed with me. It was probably cheaper keeping me than trying to sell all my stuff. She had a talking-to with me after that morning and we worked out a compromise. I listened, she talked, I promised, we stayed together, it never happened again. Some compromise. When we got married, we both said that we couldn't change and neither one of us expected to change the other. So we got married. I changed my ways, she didn't. Same kind of compromise, I guess.

The Pirates Of Penance

While this could make a chapter all by itself, it really belongs here, within this chapter, because it's all about users. In the beginning, sharing was a part of computers, because we shared everything, even the programs that we did ourselves. Hell, it was only typing. Most of the stuff, we copied in from the magazines that sold it to us. So everybody was typing in all that they could and we swapped it on a weekly basis. These sessions gave us programs that we savored. One of which, Arlene the Good, Arlene the Pure, talks about to this day. I think it was called "Santa Paravia," written by George Blank for Radio Shack's TRS-80, Model I and II (I recently found the text version of it restored on the web into a Mac OS X variation, believe it or not - 1979 version.) Before the Zork stuff. You had your little Italian Fiefdom and attempted to rise up to become a King and Queen, but only if you ruled intelligently and well. You had to overcome famine and pestilence, war and tributes and all that kind of stuff, and the game took half of forever. That's where you really learned to SAVE, and often, for the game was re-written in Apple BASIC. God knows how long it took us to type it in. We must have typed in that code dozens of times before it worked consistently. We spent many hours together playing that game, many wonderful hours, just the two of us, and the computer.

Sharing software was okay then. Some programs came out that were advertised in the magazines that someone bought and passed around. Not expensive, like under ten dollars or so. Some were worthless and some were quite enjoyable. Eventually they became more professional and more expensive to buy. Not a lot of us could afford it. Or even use it, to be more precise. It was just the thrill of seeing it that was the enjoyment of it all. I remember the first time that I saw VisiCalc. I was amazed with it. I copied it. PIRATED IT, if you will. Just to have it. To look at, to play with. Did I use it? Nope. Would I use it? Nope. Play with? Yep. Showed it to others, who then bought it? Yep! I even demo'd a VisiCalc copy one night that almost sold a dozen copies the next day in the store. It was my pirated copy I demo'd. Did I feel guilty? Nope. I justified it by thinking I was an unpaid sales person for VisiCalc. I never used it for any real work that I did. Just for playing with for showing to people. A couple of companies bought Apple computers after I showed them a VisiCalc demo.

Shortly after, Microsoft copied (re-engineered) the whole darn thing and brought out Excel. I guess Brickland never copyrighted or patented the software to begin with. Bill Gates did NOT make that mistake. So why would I feel guilty? I'm sure that Bill Gates sleeps well at night. Does he feel guilty? Software wasn't patented in those early days. It was treated as a mathematical thing, not a tangible thing. Only later on did software become eligible for patents.

After the Macintosh came out and software eventually came out for the end users, copying was big time. I participated, in the early days, even for stuff that I didn't want, just because I could! You had to be there! It was like 'the time and the place.' Like when the hippies were doing drugs. Yeah, it was illegal, but everybody was doing it, man. You know what I mean. Fortunately, the people in our group weren't doing drugs, we couldn't afford it. We owned Apple computers now. Our money was spent on having a different sort of high, an Apple High! Hidey Ho, neighbors! We were all so Apple-centric, we didn't notice much that went on around us. Our free time was spent on this great thing we were doing. And sharing. Together. The Apple Owners User Group. The beginning of a something that continues to this day. That today is a national sharing.

Arlene and I moved a couple of times, and even then, we moved into an Apple User Group. Different people, different leaders, but still a common theme. Helping each other to become better at what you want to do with your Apple computer. Different groups, common theme, to this day. Our current group has the motto "People, Helping People." That's what it's about. Most Mac people have evolved from the Pirates thing. Almost all the Mac people I know now buy their software that they use. Occasionally, someone will say "Look at this XYZ software, it's great!" Would they use it? Could they afford it? Nope! Do they use it in any productive manner? Nope! Have they sold more legal copies of the software by showing the pirated software? Probably so. A lot of software companies got their real start by having their stuff flouted and copied about. VisiCalc, Microsoft, FileMaker, Zork, and some of the gaming industry great names of today and yesterday. I'm not condoning the illegal copying of those days, just stating what I saw and believed. Today, I own my legal FileMakers, Pagemaker and Photoshops', because I use and enjoy them daily, and take great pleasure in doing so. However, would I spend that great a dollar on a program like that without a 'trial' copy first. I don't think so. And neither does a great many other people. Most software copying is done in the PC world, much more so than in the Mac world. So if the Software Publishers Association wants to piss and moan, they're in the wrong stall, in my opinion. Talk to the PC users, not the Mac people. Mac vendors of software programs mostly have 'Tryout' versions of their more expensive programs that expire in thirty days or more. If you like it, call them and order it. It's that easy. ADOBE, that grand old Lady of the industry, recognized the problem and dealt with it in a mature way. Try it. See if you like it. They have a protection feature that's responsible and acceptable to the end user. Try it, you'll like it!

I just think that Microsoft is doing things the wrong way, but that's just my personal feeling. You don't go out with your whole legal division and threaten to sue everybody that uses your software illegally. People take this as a challenge, and Americans love challenges. Take the Napster thing. The Music Industry bought the Politicians and the laws that made Napster illegal. When the public found out about it, they got kind of upset that they couldn't copy what they bought, without the Music Industry fighting them about it. Kind of like the VCR thing all over again. So now the people are going about copying their music, and everybody else's music, with a vengeance. Almost like the American thing with the Tea Tax! Now the politicians are in a quandary about what to do or say. You can't put the genie back in the bottle. I'm not a music listener, don't own an iPod and probably never will. It doesn't interest me that much. Wrong generation, I guess. AND, I will NOT buy a $400 or $500 product, with a built-in Hard Drive from Apple with a 90 day (now a one year) warranty. NEVER! Remember, I do this for a living. I know what a hard drive does. I know how it works. Anything that rotates at 4,500 revolutions a minute or more and has the microscopic head clearances that a hard drive has while writing and reading data, AND is MOBILE while doing it, is not something that has only a 90-day warranty. I'm sorry, folks. That's the techie in me speaking out.

All this technology makes copying so easy today, that the Entertainment Industry has a losing battle on it's hands. If they win it in the courts, they'll lose it in the streets, and over the airwaves and Internet. They have to change their way of thinking, like ADOBE. Be flexible. Adapt your way of thinking. Find a new way, one that won't antagonize the users. Let the User's help you to succeed, like with iTunes. It worked for Apple. It still helps Apple today, in spite of their dumb commercials.

So what makes these Apple people band together like lemmings headed for the sea? Who leads the groups? What kind of person does it take to do this? I feel that I can speak out for some User Group people in general. I've met, talked with and dallied with User Group leaders from across this wide country over the span of twenty-five years now. I started my love affair with the Apple platform in 1979 and haven't left it since. I'm considered an old veteran in many users eyes. Each Apple User Group has to elect an Executive Board to oversee the efficient running of the group, from the financial end to the meetings themselves. If the meetings aren't interesting or Theme'd properly, you'll lose attendance and eventually the Group will fail. You have to have Help Groups, or sessions, to help the new users out there, or they will leave also. You also have Special Interest Groups for interests like Graphics, Digital Cameras, FileMaker, writing seminars, music and the like. If you're REAL lucky, you just might find someone who has a real interest in one of these topics and will lead the interest group into a successful string of meetings. Serving on an Executive Board is a dubious honor. It means many nights of phone calls, writing, planning and organizing people and events so they might, just might, come together successfully as you planned it.

Sometimes it means swallowing your pride and letting others do what you most want to do, because that's the way to keep that person on the Board. Delegating is the hardest thing to do as a Board President, especially if you've done all the rest of the positions on the Board, because you feel as if you know what has to be done, so why not do it. Even when it's done not as well as you'd do it yourself. Then you have to praise the do'er for a job well (sic) done. Eventually, you'll have a well run Executive Board, where anyone on the Board can do any other position.

Most importantly, as an Executive Board Member, you have to be able to put aside your personal ego and help decide what's best for the group at large, not just yourself or your personal friends. There's no 'I' in User Group. It's a hard thing to do at times, but you can't take things personally when votes don't go the way you want them to go. It's the vote of the majority and you have to put aside that damn ego of yours and pull for that majority decision, even it it's against what you believe to be the right thing. That's difficult, my friends. Boards can split up because of decisions like that. If you see something like that coming, divert the discussion away from a vote. Delay, delay, delay, if at all possible. And tell the Board why you're delaying it. Let the cooler heads prevail. I've seen much larger groups run like fiefdoms and dissolve after awhile. Nobody was allowed to do anything. The head cheese wanted to do it all 'his' way. Big mistake, as User Groups depend on volunteers. In most groups, volunteers recognize their duty just in time to avoid it. Here, it's our lifeline. Find the person who least wants the position of President and cajole him or her into the job. Then support the hell out of that person. Give them everything they need to lessen the impact of the job on them. You'll keep that person and they'll be effective for the group.

The next strongest person, besides the Treasurer, is the Greeter. The what? You heard me right. The Greeter. The person at the door who says hello; who takes care of the sign-in sheet; who takes care of the raffle items and the 50-50 raffle. This is the first person new people see when they come in the door and usually the last out the door. This has to be an extremely extroverted and bubbly person who really enjoys people contact and rarely gets ruffled. We're extremely lucky with our greeter and have had her as Greeter and Board member for over ten years. If you can find one like that, keep them at ALL costs. Whatever it takes. That job is almost as important, if not as important, as the President's position.

Having taken almost every position there is and ever was in User Group positions and Executive Board's, I realize how difficult and trying a job it is to be a President of one. I had the job a couple of times and was glad when it was over. I considered it a two-part job. One part is overseeing the Executive Board and the other is the effective running of the User Group. The President is governing at the discretion of the members! You have to remember that, to keep your ego and humility under control. You're serving the members, not in charge of them. It's a symbiotic relationship, where your job gets easier when they're happiest. When you give your Board members more control of their own destiny, they're happier. Keep feeding them what they need to do their job, even if you think you can do the job better than they can. Let them do it! Delegate! The whole is more important than any one individual.

Another thing I realized as President and as a long-term serving Board member in many groups, is the diversity of the memberships. There are so many Mac people from so many different walks of life. Members want to do so many different things. In the old days it was different. No one knew anything. Today, there are so many different levels of expertise that the typical User Group has to try and meet everyones' needs. It's an impossible task. We used to try and have a greeter meet new people and have the greeter partner the newcomer with an experienced person when they sit down for the meeting. Try and hold their hand, so to speak. I wish that were possible today. I don't know why that was stopped. Maybe because of the lack of volunteers.

It's harder today to get vendors to come to meetings, due to tighter fiscal restraints. When you do get speakers, even from the Group itself, what topics do you want to talk about? A show of hands? 3x5 cards for input? We tried them all. One thing I decided to do a demo on is digital cameras, since everyone was buying them. What kind of printer would you buy to go along with that camera? Ahah, another topic. Which leads to what software would you use to edit and play with those pictures? There's another topic for a demo. Sometimes you just say to hell with it and use your own judgment, based on what you think sounds like a great approach to get into your members minds. You can't please each and every one of your members at the same meeting with the same demo. Hopefully they won't start a conversation during your presentation. I try to keep it fun and energized, as well as entertaining, with lots of oooh's and ahhh's during the way. One of the best at this is Terry White, one of Adobe's bright and shining stars. I just love to see that man work at a presentation. Very witty and bright.

On our Board, part of my contribution to my peer Board members was my Mac Service expertise in the beginning. I was available to anyone on the Executive Board, day or night. As long as I was home. If I was in the shop, it had to be paid service, of course. Wearing two hats wasn't easy over the years. At User Group meetings, members could ask me any questions on Macs or service problems. I was popular in the early years and our 'dog and pony' help sessions were very helpful in getting full attendance. That was before the Internet became useful and popular. At our highest peak, we had over 650 members on our database. Of course, what you had on your database and what you had for attendance was a different thing. For EVERY Apple User Group.

We give our Executive Board members free membership in lieu of their time and many phone calls they make without billing the group. We've been very lucky with our Newsletter Editors over the years. I'm a very graphic-oriented person and have been instrumental in making that luck, I'm happy to say. Whatever it takes, I'll do it, to get a good newsletter out the door. That's the first thing that people see of a group. That's advertising, folks. That's what we are and this is what we do. Keeping your leaders of the group focused and happy is what will keep that group going over the long haul. Recognizing when the lead horse is tired and ready for replacement is very important. No more than two years in the lead traces is our motto. You get burned out. Give someone else a chance in the spotlight. Always be on the lookout for new blood. Suck them in any way you can. How about a nice, brand new, unopened copy of 'XYZ' to review? Yep, Board members get chances and first shots like that, as long as they're willing to do a demo and software review of it. Home phone numbers of people to help you out of a bind - okay! Can't do this month's newsletter? Okay, I'll back you up! That's what it's about, folks. People… helping People. Notice I capitalize both ends of the people equation? Both sides are just as important. I guess people of a kind flock together just like birds or wildebeest, for survival. And just as in the wild, the User Group Leaders are very important for a successful migration.

CHAPTER 13

The EXPO's

Note that I used all Capital letters when I used the word Expo above. If you haven't been to a Mac Expo yet, go to one. You owe it to yourself to see what all those crazed people are like all in one place. Now, my idea of a fun place is not the Javits Center in New York. I know, I know, New York City people are going to blast me for it, but all the same, it's not the same as being in the original city of Boston, folks, for a great time. Even more so for a family.

A note for all you New York City people that are starting to write me hate letters about "you don't know about..." etc., etc. I'm a native New York State'r by birth and lived in New York most of my life. I lived In Yonkers, New Rochelle, all over Long Island and the hated Long Island Expressway and associated parkways, and Upstate New York. I worked in New York City day and night for almost twelve years, working with construction people and working in most of the Hospitals in the X-Ray Service Industry for most of that time. There's not much you can tell me about New York City. I've seen the worst and the best. I can deal with the Times Square crowd and the Theater District crowd. I love New York City and I hate it both. I loved Harlem and the Bowery both, as well as the flavor of Canal Street, Mott Street and Little Italy. In most cases, you just leave the people alone and they leave you alone. Everybody has their own business to do. Don't mess with people and they'll leave you alone. There are memories that stay with you all the time. My Servicemen had to deal with the muggers and the City Hospitals in all of the boroughs. As long as you look forward, neither left nor right, and attend to your business, you can deal with New Yorkers.

A quick example for you die-harder's in the CITY. For you non-native New York people, the CITY is what New York City people refer to themselves as. (You mean there is another?) I was in the CITY with my wife one night to take in a Victor Borge night at the theater. An extremely competent and funny man, by the way. We had stopped for a traffic light, which immediately made us for out-of-town'ers, when a pedestrian right next to us started to jaywalk across the street against the light. A taxicab started to make a turn from the street to the left of us and knocked the man down. Not bleeding, but he couldn't get up. Not one person lent to give him a hand. Now everybody saw it happen, but not one person stopped or looked down at him! I can't think of any other city in the United States where that kind of thing could happen. And that's not a once-in-a-lifetime occurrence, folks. Remember, I worked there for a long time. New Yorkers kind of expect that and don't want to get involved.

Another example? Sure. My wife, Arlene the Pure, Arlene the Good, was walking home from her Karate class when she was living in Manhattan, around 125th and Amsterdam. She was a single mother at the time, supporting her child and herself by working at Columbia College. Arlene was carrying her Karate clothes bag with her and three thugs attempted to mug her. She kicked one, who later ran away, and disabled the other two a little more seriously. Across the street, two guys were sitting on the stoop (front steps for you non-New Yorkers) of a building watching it all. Upset at their nonchalance and un-gentlemanly behavior to a woman in need, she walked across the street and asked them "why didn't you help me?" Their reply was "Lady, you was doin' all right by ya'self." New York attitude, I guess. That bag was all the valuables she owned. She couldn't afford to buy more clothes for her karate class. Plus, she was ex-Marine and pissed. Bad mistake on their part. But, she left the muggers laying there, so I guess she was as New Yorker as the on-lookers were. Needless to say, have I made my point to you native New York City people who are reading this chapter?

My first Expo was in Boston. The first Expo was so large in attendance that they had to hold it in two parts of the city. The big guys, like Microsoft, Claris and those kinds of guys were in one part and the Gamers, Utilities guys and the like were in another part; MY part. It was an awesome event. We always saved the big guys till last. The fun part was the first day. All the little guys were there. The little game companies and start-up companies all showed their wares. They could afford to. It was much cheaper than New York City. Casady & Green always had their products there. Parsoft's A-10 flight simulator program was introduced there with the pilot doing the demo in an actual A-10 ejector seat dressed in his flight G-suit and all three VERY LARGE working monitors. That day all the BIG flight programs demo'd there to great crowds. The Berkeley AFTER DARK crowd, Connectix, Aladdin, all the best known names and all the newcomers showed up to share in the spotlight.

The crowds ooh'd and ahh'd and touched and peeped and played with everything that they could and spent, spent and spent. It was a cacophony of sound, with everyone shouting their wares. It was a shoulder-to-shoulder crowd of pushing and shoving people. Those Boston Expo's were also home to the days that UMAX and those crazy people from POWER COMPUTING were selling their Macintosh Clones. Some of the best Mac advertisements EVER came from Power Computing. Their booths were always a crazy place to be around. T-Shirt raffles, CPU give-away's one a day, etc., and other demos and goodies to lure the unwary. Yep, they were always there, folks. God, it was so exciting!

And for those out-of-town'ers, the good old Expo BBBB's, the Busty Blonde Booth Bimbos. It was hard to keep your mind on other things when around every corner was someone like "Come on in, fill this out, win a..." Give me a break, wilya? That's a New York City word, folks. WILYA. I asked directions from a New Yorker once, and was told "Two blocks straight ahead and make a right on 14th, wilya?" All in a loud and verbally aggressive reply. Then he kept walking! What the hell kind of response was that? Again and again people would use that word. No other city I've visited or lived in have I heard that word since. Weird! Back to the Expo...

My favorite place was Boston as an Expo site. Once they cleaned up the "Combat Zone," Boston's challenge to Philadelphia to be called a City of Love, it was a family place where you didn't worry about being out at night. There was so much to see and do after hours, it was great. The seafood was phenomenal, maybe second to San Francisco, maybe not. The Aquarium was great. Faneuil Hall was a must-see as a food-sorting extravaganza. Great story behind that place. Go there to find out more about it. Cooking of all kinds of Nationalities in there. And outside, there were clowns, musicians and shows to watch while you sit and have your lunch. If you have a mind to, drop some change in their hat to pay for their performance. We stayed out of town and shared a room. We all did. Usually twenty or more of us, caravans of cars and vans showed up at the Red Roof Inn, or a similar place, and shared rooms at $49 or $59 a night. Split two ways, it was cheaper than Boston, and only a twenty minute ride away. Well worth the inconvenience. After the second time there, we found the away-from-traffic places to go for food and value, like the time-honored 'Callahans.' Great food, dessert and a movie ticket for less than fifteen dollars. Whoa! And the movies were VERY clean, and spacious, and NEW! Oh yeah! Do I miss it? You can say that again! Finish up the night with a Dunkin Donuts donut and a Starbucks coffee and then back to the room for "Hive Time."

"Hive Time" was when we gathered in someone's room (pick one), and talked about the Vendors and goodies and things that we saw and missed. Everyone gathered around and ooh'd and ahh'd as someone brought out their software or hardware or gimmick or stupid 'gimme" that they acquired during the show, and where they got it. Notes were exchanged, promises were made as to where we'd meet the following day, and what times we were going to meet and where at, etc. It was our "Hive Time." Something that was not to be when moved to New York City and the Javits Center. It just wasn't that friendly outside of Boston. Boston's Expo was an attitude!

When the move to NYC took place, letters of complaining response to the move were sent in to the exhibitors, etc., all to no avail. The show goes on! In Javits, I noticed that the smaller booth exhibitors that we loved in Boston just weren't there anymore. In talking to some of the old exhibitors, they said they just couldn't afford the Javits and NYC expenses. 'Off the record' responses, of course. They still advertised in MacWorld. Some of them were my favorite software people. I missed them very much. They drew good traffic.

How about the food? Expo food is still expensive and you're foolish if you try and eat inside Javits. I did, the first year and boy, was it a mistake! Dried sandwiches, bottled soda, VERY expensive and long lines! Want a great hint, my friends? Just outside the Javits Center, across the street, are those little wheeled carts that have the most tasty hot dogs in this universe! Hot dogs with peppers and onions, you name it, and only about $1.50 each. A couple of those and an ice-cold Pepsi or Snapple and you have a dynamite lunch break. Just sit in the sunshine on a bench or table, or just sit on the steps and watch the passers-by, as other CITY people do. It's a great way to save money and taste the ethnic CITY snack food. If you do travel up near Central Park later in the colder season, you just have to try the hot chestnut stands in season. Man, they're good. I'm ramblin… again. Back to the Expo.

At the last Expo I went to in New York, all my old User Group cronies were there, and I enjoyed the people part of it very much. The old faces in the old places. At almost every Expo, there's a User Group Room that used to be called the UGWUMP room, that User Group members use for rest and relaxation from the mad pace of the day. You can drop your baggage and rest your tired feet. We used to meet there at designated times of the day just in case we missed an important place or item that was just introduced. One of those "DID-JASEE" things! WOW! You know what I mean. Almost always, we'd bring a couple of months samples of our newsletters and drop them on the tables, along with many other User Group's samples. It became a tradition that continues to this day. Fred Showker was usually in charge of setting up the User Group Awards ceremonies for best whatevers, like best newsletters, best web sites, etc., and it was always a charge to be selected by your peers as outstanding anything. Fred is an outstanding person in his own right. A real classy guy, and a talented Newsletter and Design guy. He's done a lot for the User Group people over the years and never had his due, nor wanted any. Fred, you're a class act! Just in case it never comes around again!

There are a lot of people who make Expo's happen; and User Groups happen. Carmella Zamorra, now married, has always been one of the User Group people who loves people, and still follows through at all the Expo's to help User Group members over the hump, so to speak. People like these are one of the reasons that I still go, year after year. The thrill isn't the same anymore, like it used to be. The excitement is still okay and the crowds are smaller, but still there. I've noticed that the pizzazz is missing somehow. Maybe I'm getting older, or wiser, or immune to the huckster-ism and showboat-ism, or maybe I'm just at the point where I've seen so much new stuff lately that I'm worn out. Maybe I have to take a year or two off the Merry-Go-Round and re-invigorate myself. My love for the Macs and the User Groups have never waned, as does my love for life on the Service Bench itself. I love the anticipation of the next service problem, the next unknown, the next service call on the line. Yeah, I'll miss it all when I finally hang up my test prods. Some Day... but not yet!

Notice that I said I enjoyed the people part very much. The recent show part was atrocious. In years past, you could take three days and still miss things. Since it was at Javits in New York, you could do it all in two days and you might miss some things. I've noticed that in the past couple of years, we've seen it all in just one day. This year we arrived and toured the whole Mac Expo in just two hours! We arrived at the Javits doors, after driving four and a half hours and checking in at the hotel, at around eleven in the morning. By two in the afternoon, I was outside at the wheeled snack stand with my Pepper and Onions hot dog and Snapple, wondering what the hell it was that I could have missed. After a long and leisurely 'sit down' on the steps across the street eating my cheap lunch, I discovered that this has been happening over the years. Less people are showing up to see the new stuff and the Javits people were closing off more and more wings with less floor space for exhibitors. All my favorite exhibitors were not showing up anymore, and if they did, they were only showing a small booth with a few limited demos. When asked, they admitted the financial strain of New York was just too much for them anymore. Two said they weren't coming to New York next year. Ouch!

When IDG said that the Expo was going to be in Boston next year, our User Group applauded that decision. However, Steve Jobs said that Apple wouldn't be going if it was going to be held in Boston. HE wanted New York! As far as he was concerned, it was New York or nothing. Ego, Ego, Ego. Putting himself above what's good for the company! IDG is adamant on this one, folks. It WILL be in Boston, with or without Apple (at this time). It looks like Apple is loading their gun again to shoot themselves in the foot. This decision can only hurt Apple. I will NOT be going to another NY Expo again. Last year it appeared to be less than half of the year before, and Apple can't see it as a financial decision of the vendors. Very myopic, if you ask me. But then again, it's been a long time since Apple has been concerned over the struggles of it's vendors. I guess that's 'their problem!'

I really miss those good old times. But then again, I guess we can all say the same thing about lots of things in our younger days. Luckily, our mind tunes out and in time, forgets the bad memories in our past. Now if I was a drinking man, I'd probably say this was the perfect time in our travels to take a break, find a friendly place and a table, and have a drink or two for times, friends and memories in the past. Salud!

Real User Friendly, too!!

Nice Bits!

The Service Department - Part I

In the beginning, my servicing concept was based on my years as an IBM Service Engineer with Mainframes, Card Punches, Tele-Processing and Typewriter divisions. Dress the role and walk the Talk. Neat, everything in order, paperwork processed properly, all the equipment you worked on was properly engineered and diagrams for everything. Then, later on in my X-Ray days, most of that was continued. Engineered properly, European equipment from Germany, Holland, France and the like, where Engineering held sway like Gods. Perfection ruled, most of the time. Then I got involved with American X-Ray companies, where we innovated, many times on the fly. We made changes like babies diapers. On the manufacturing line. Something was better, we incorporated it. Lots of times, after the manufacturer did; right on the test beds, or on the customers set-up line, where we set up the customers equipment for pre-installation site testing. We made modifications all the time, but we always made proper changes on schematics so they, and we, knew all about it. That was on-the-fly engineering and I loved the excitement of it.

But in the personal computer field, things were a lot different. NO schematics were available from the PC Manufacturers. But then again, putting a schematic in the hands of some of those technicians would be like putting a loaded gun in the hands of an idiot. But, I wanted schematics! I wanted to be able to do board-level diagnostics. I had one of my degrees in Engineering. I wanted to do my thing! MY way. It was not to be. At least, doing it their way. So I cheated, I reverse-engineered and scrounged up diagrams from wherever I could to do the jobs the best way I could. I wanted to excel at my work. I wanted to be the best. I wanted the customers to come to me with their problems and I wanted to solve ALL of them. I was the quintessential Service Engineer! I had to be the best, at least in my own mind. I had my ideas of what a Service Department should be, and the Service Technicians that ran it should be like me, where the customer got only the best advice from you. Remember, I was IBM Service trained in my early days, and I carried that idea with me for almost twenty five years before I got into the personal computer field; full time, for good. So I had a mindset that was almost set in stone. Unfortunately, that mindset was a lot different than the mindset of what the Dealer Sales people were used to.

When I started in this business, the store I worked in, part-time, was being ripped off by service people who were not professional by any stretch of the imagination. In a short period of time, the owners relied on my judgment and the other people weren't there any more. I did my best work, but we did Apple and PC both. Yes, folks, I actually did work on PC's! I have to admit it. I actually was paper certified to work on a number of manufacturers CPU's. IBM, Compaq and a slew of others. I liked Apple the best, because it was the coolest! AND, the fastest to service! Keep that in mind, folks, The fastest! Because it keeps coming back to play in what molded me into my Apple Service philosophy.

The Sales Department Manager liked to make money, and that's as it should be. His philosophy was that the Corporations he sold to had to get their equipment from him, come what may. If that meant selling at a few points over cost, then that's what he had to do. He made it up in the peripherals. Many times, and at the end, he gave away the installations and setups as a 'gimme.' Part of the cost of doing business. The Service Department was just another tool in the salesman's bag of tricks. Eventually, all kinds of promises were made that we couldn't keep. As the Service Manager, I was being put between the Customer, the Sales Manager and his people and the Service Department. I couldn't tell the customer the truth, which is that the sales people lied to them. I couldn't tell my service people that they were being screwed by the sales people lying about them. And I couldn't tell the sales people that my service people were laughing at them for selling crap that would NEVER work right! In the end, it was the customer that was being screwed left and right.

When that company was taken over by a conglomerate, The Computer Factory, I finally had my chance to do it right. I went to the New York Corporate office and was hired as the Service Manager for that store. I hired the right Service staff and proceeded to do things as I felt they should be done. I answered to Corporate and operated as a service 'profit center.' No more freebies! Warranty service was paid for by the Manufacturers and was put in the service departments books as income, not the sales department. I made my service people feel good by giving THEM a commission for selling warranties on the computer products. At one point, our small store did over a quarter million dollars in AppleCare contracts, outselling 65 other stores around the country. We continued outselling most of the stores for the life of the chain. However, the Sales Manager felt that the commissions belonged to his department. Sorry, Charley, talk to Corporate. My department was in very good shape, profit-wise. Continually in the top 3-4 in the Corporate chain. Even though it was maybe one-third the size of the larger New York City stores. We had a lot of pride in our work. What really helped is that we were charging for set-ups now, and for that, the sales staff got a commission, because it was on the order. However, the Service Department got a little taste also. Life was good. In the education market, the Apple computers were king. The Dealers Education Sales people had a good life there. Very little competition and lots of service work for our department. LOTS of work! In a short period of time, we were becoming a very noted source of quick, fast, Apple Macintosh Service people. Macs were being turned around in half an hour for major board replacements. Done and out the door. While you wait service! We actually had lots of out-of-state service UPS'd to us, which was faster than their local repair centers could service. This didn't sit too well with our Sales Manager, as we weren't doing his PC-Centric work that fast. DUH!

On the PC side; remember in those days that it was a hodge-podge world where marriages were made in hell, DOS things just didn't work as advertised. Sales people were selling cards from this manufacturer and that manufacturer and it was our job to make it all work. Many, many calls had to made to the Card manufacturers to get the proper settings to make things work, if they ever did, and sometimes we had to tell the salespeople to sell the customer something else. And, who's going to pay us for the time we spent? Uh oh, trouble in the air now...

Luckily, Corporate had phone numbers for everything. Problems came up, I passed it on and continued generating money for the company. Enough so, that I did quite well in bonuses and compensation for all the service contracts we generated. I guess that continued to be a sore point for years with the sales department, for that kept coming up. My service people were VERY happy in that they were now being compensated for their extra-curricular sales activities.

I always believed that a good, competent Service Engineer could sell something if he deeply believed in it. I proved it then, because my people believed in themselves and their own competency enough so, that they could sell Apple Service Contracts easily. We were turning them around in just half an hour! I proved my point to my people one day after hours by turning off the lights, 'cracking' the MacPlus case open, and disconnecting the Power Supply/Video Board, replacing the Board, reconnecting the connections and High Voltage CRT connector (a little sting there) and putting the case all back together, in just twenty-five minutes, in total darkness! My legend was born! Corporate learned about that (not from me) and it was spread from store to store, with others trying it. One service techie from one of the California stores called me and said that he was finally able to do it also. His store also had a great service volume, mostly Mac, no surprise to me. So needless to say, our techies were great, we had a lot of self-confidence and we respected each others abilities. Unfortunately, the turnaround time for the then-DOS machines were very slow. Slow DOS System install times, around two hours or more, not counting peripheral RAM or Video or Modem cards. Oh, you want your programs installed? More cost, more time. Time is money. Now the Sales Department was starting to see the value of all that Service Time that was freely given away before. I was justified in my way of doing things. Our Mac sales were increasing all the time. Our Service Team was, in effect, the best sales force that the company could have asked for. Many times, our knowledgeable customers would come back and ask us what equipment they should buy. We would tell them when they were being over-sold, or when they were being given a bill-of-goods. They would then go back up front and order what they then felt was right. Less time for the sales people; just write up the order. However, the Sales Manager felt offended. I felt it was not my problem, and I guess it partly was, looking back on it. I felt more attuned to the customer, being the Mac person that I am. I knew when they were being taken advantage of. And they were, but that's business.

At that point I decided, if I ever have a chance to have my own business, it would be a Service Business where I would do what's right for the customer, to hell with the manufacturer and the Sales People involved. Do what's right, and the customers will come to you.

Unfortunately, fate was moving in just that direction. Corporate was having it's own share of hell and started closing their stores, a block at a time. From 65 or so, down to 45, then 25, then it was our turn. Gradually, they started requesting 'excess' store service inventory being returned to Corporate. Well, says I, let's define Excess. In my parlance, I wanted more inventory, as I was turning around Macs like nobody's business, and had the numbers, and dollars, to prove it. My numbers bought me lots of time, and requests for favors from other service managers, for emergency store transfers on special cases. Eventually, though, their problems escalated with their Vendors, like Apple and IBM, etc. in that they weren't getting their parts like they used to. Payment problems started escalating to Apple and the other vendors, and I started getting my parts, not from Apple, but from Corporate, that were repaired by others than Apple. Uh-oh, you can see where this is going! People with AppleCare warranties started to have problems with their replacement boards that were NOT Apple certified replacement boards, and I could NOT state the truth, not exactly! And I knew the truth. Sometimes I repaired the 'repaired' boards prior to letting them leave my shop for replacement. It started to go downhill from there. Then Corporate wanted ALL my parts back. They would send them overnight, they said! Uh-oh again. Danger signals. Within the next couple of months, we weren't able to complete our repairs, and daily calls escalated, from customers to sales to corporate. One morning we came in and the doors were closed and we were met by security, who let us take our personal stuff out the door. That was the end of the road for The Computer Factory in this region.

I continued doing some service work on my own for awhile, before hooking up with another large chain and doing regional work for them on a continued basis with a small store front for awhile. But it wasn't the real answer. I knew what the answer for me was, but at my age of fifty, it was a real challenge, one that I didn't want to make. I never worked for myself, never. Could I do it? I guess Arlene the Good, Arlene the Pure had more faith in me than I did, because she really goosed me to get it on. Talk about the Golden Goose...! Go for it!

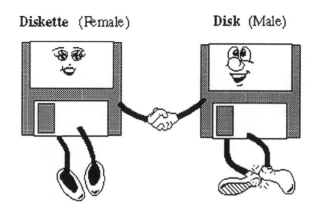

Diskette (Female)   Disk (Male)

CHAPTER 15

The Service Department - Part II

Starting your own business at the age of fifty would be a nightmare for most folks. It wasn't so much a nightmare as it was a necessity for me. We had to have money, and this was the thing that I wanted to do. There was a need for it, as no other Mac Service was available in the area, and I was the only one with the incentive and the 'good hands' to do it. So I started doing it, right out of the house. It started small, like sex. Gradually, it improved to the point where my wife started complaining. The business, not the sex. Or, was it the other way around? Either way, it kept growing. The harder we worked at it, the longer the hours it took out of the day. Finally, one day, Arlene the Good, Arlene the Pure, came home and found nineteen computers, monitors and printers in her living room. Most were finished and waiting for customers to pick up. However, it was a showdown kind of day. In her own sweet lovable way, it was kind of a 'them' or 'us' kind of thing. She wanted her house back. I understand. Mac men understand that kind of thing. Mac women kind of hold something over your head, if you get my drift. So I concurred and looked hard for a place. REAL hard. Within a week, we found a place in a shopping center where we had the traffic that I wanted, on the off chance I was going to do Mac Sales. However, in my mind, that wasn't a real possibility.

Why, does one ask? One could answer, in the third person, of course, that a customer might just question why a service person would tell them that a unit was not really recommended for repair. Then show them the latest Apple computer at an especially good price. I know what I'd think. So, over the years, I kind of stayed with that philosophy. A real good Service Department should be able to stand on it's own merits and make a profit without outside Macintosh sales. We've done it for seventeen years so far, but the times are starting to show.

Apple requires people to send their PowerBooks and iBooks back to Apple for repair now, instead of bringing it to an Apple Dealer. The same goes for some of their other products. Less service revenue for Dealers, more for Apple. Of course, one repair we could have done for $24.00 in parts and $60 labor, Apple charged the customer $329.00. Bingo. The customer said her next computer was going to be a Dell. Unfortunately, she did buy a Dell laptop a year later. While Apple makes great laptops, their in-house repair policies and pricing for same are turning people off to Apple. More and more people are going into PC laptops. Forget the fact that the PowerBooks and iBooks are prettier, look nicer and have a GREAT OS. Remember, folks, OS X is a UNIX based OS. Guess what? UNIX is freeware based software and it's only a matter of time before the Mac OS and Windows and a UNIX-based pretty face OS comes about. Then the PowerBook is dead, as a standalone unit. Of course, that's just my opinion, and I'm an old guy who doesn't know much. Ask any one of my kids.

Back to the bench! So now you know my philosophy, and my rambling habits. Did you know that I've been doing a 24 year column almost every month for User Groups, presently called "Ramblin...?" Well, now you do. I guess I just ramble on about whatever comes into my mind at any one time. Sometimes it's scary stuff. In fact, my wife says it's now most of the time.

Back to the Bench! For awhile, after including Toner Cartridge refilling services as part of my work, I was busy six to seven days a week, starting at nine in the morning and often coming home as late as three the next morning. It's what you had to do. Gradually, one of my sons came into the business with me and that really helped with the hours. I did a lot of on-site calls early on in the business. Over time, that had to stop. It just wasn't cost-effective anymore. In the shop, I could work on three units simultaneously. Between the two of us, we could have six units on the benches and be effective and it would be cost-effective for the customer also. To give an example, I could start running diagnostic software on one unit, be cleaning out a printer at the same time, then start diagnostics on a third unit while the first was running. Go back to the first unit, do software work, and possibly a second level of diagnostics, go to the third unit, do a 'Clean Install,' clean the printer up, do the service invoice, put it up front for pickup, put another on the bench, etc. Rotating my time all day like that. While the diagnostics were running, the service time clock mentally stops for that customer and machine. We don't charge all the customers for the same time. That's unethical in my mind, but most shops do it all the time. Pad the bill. It's on the bench, so it's Bench Time as long as it's there, whether they're actively looking at it or not. We just couldn't work that way! I have to face Arlene the Good, Arlene the Pure. Here's a ramblin... thought that just comes to mind. When I married Arlene the Good, she told me, "...if I ever catch you lying to me, the marriage is over." Whoooooeeee! I promised, and never went back on my word, to the best of my recollection. So, I guess I always think of something like that when I work on a customers bill. Is it right? Can I justify this price? There are times when we make a software mistake and have to do it over again. The customer is never charged for that time when we goof up. That's on our plate, not theirs.

   We have some close friends over the years that just like to stop by and chat, and we invite some of them to the back of the shop to sit back and rest for a bit while we work. We CAN do that and be effective, believe it or not. Some customers like to come back, uninvited. We try to discourage that by a number of ways. Sometimes we tell them that it makes us slower, because we then have to explain some things to them, and it could double the price of a repair. One time my son started typing away and throwing things away at an incredible pace, faster than even I could follow, and the customer said she couldn't follow what he was doing. No shit, Sherlock! I couldn't either! Anyway, he asked her to 'wait a minute, until he finished what he was doing.' Then while the Trash was emptying, he said 'did she want an explanation?' At $60.00 per hour, all the things he emptied required an in-depth explanation of how the Operating System worked, and the things that he found wrong with each of those items. It would take at least two more hours for him to sit and show her just that on a whiteboard. Would that be worth the additional $120.00? She didn't think so and didn't bother him again for the duration of the fast software fix. That was a quickie repair. Normally, the customer isn't invited. Only when it requires input from the customer, like in a network password situation, or an "It only happens when I do this…" kind of thing, do we invite a customer back into the work space. But; they all want to come back and watch us do those magical things on their computers. How to say no, how to say no, how to say no…

CHAPTER 16

The Service Department - Part III

WHAT IF WE WERE NAKED?

Ah ha! Naked Service Technicians! What a GREAT idea! So let's follow up on that thought; what if we were naked back there? Wow, what a wonderful thought! Now we'd have a reason not to have people back there. It'd be easy to say to a woman, well, I'd invite you back there, but with the Naked Technicians back there, it just wouldn't be right. Now if it was a guy, I just might say "Hey, if you want to go back there and see your computer, go right ahead. However, your technician is Naked. But he might not mind. He might even enjoy your company!" That would take care of that problem. Guys just don't do that sort of thing! Real guys get the shakes just thinking about sitting naked next to another naked guy. Brrrrrr. Women are just more communal beings than men are. I bet women could sit together naked and not think anything of it. But guys? Brrrrrrrrrr.

That would be another reason not to do an 'On-site' call. "Well gee, we would, but, we'd have to get dressed, see, and..." or "Well, we're naked right now, but on Tuesday..." On second thought, that could only work if the customer was already in the shop. Hmmm, for some of my customers, they'd probably pay an extra twenty bucks for that experience. Some of my women customers definitely would. I'd better stop this train of thought right here. My wife will be proof-reading this book, and I like to eat... and do other kinds of things!

Maybe I'll bring that 'Naked Serviceman at the Bench' thought up tomorrow at the shop and see what the guys think about it. I'll tell them that you brought it up and that I'm only passing it on. How does that sound? I'll get back to you on that...

Well, my son asked me if I'm taking my pills on time, and Matt, one of my best friends, wanted to start taking his clothes off to try it out. Seeing as he's an ex-hockey player and looks like a lineman for the Green Bay Packers who'd frighten all the children away, I decided against taking a vote on it. Besides, my son is running the business now and he'd only have me taken away by ambulance to that place with the rubber wallpaper on the walls. But what a novel idea! Naked Servicemen! It's a shame I never thought of that earlier.

Just as a passing fancy, let's ponder this for a moment. Before the padded wagon comes to take me away. I'm sure lots of you have heard of, and maybe even passed by a HOOTERS restaurant, right? I've never been in one, but have been told that there's even a reason for it's popularity. A number of magazines on the newsstands have also attained a level of popularity for the same reasons.

Now what could possibly be wrong if an entrepreneur decided to open up a nudist-centric Mac repair shop where nudist Mac Service Technicians liked to service Macs in the nude? I'm not talking about at the front desk where the customers would bring in their Macs or pick them up; just at the service part of the business. As an extreme thought process, this could be a money-maker! As long as we hired halfway decent technicians with bodies that wouldn't scare away the populace and have them coming back with torches and pitchforks in the middle of the night. You see where I'm going with this. With the proper name for this place, it would be an overnight success. But then again, my name isn't Richard; and my wife would NEVER approve. And I'll be damned if I'd let her do the interviews for hiring the naked technicians!

I'm having a great time on our walk down memory lane with you. As you can tell, I like to giggle and think to extremes a lot. I enjoy passing the time of day with my customers and friends alike. Most of the time, there's no difference between the two. The talk switches back and forth between equipment, applications and hints and tips on the latest software. My computer son has the same problem that I have. He loves to talk shop. Only he doesn't consider it a problem. I know it is! I have to force myself to stop talking about my love and hobby to my customers. I have work on the bench that has to get done.

The fun part of the business to me is the constant mental challenge of the next problem. And it is a challenge; sometimes just a small software problem and sometimes only beatable by formatting a drive or replacing it. The challenging part of our Service business is that we have to ALWAYS fix it, no matter what. There MUST be a resolution, or end solution to the problem. We can't just tell the customer that we don't know how to fix their problem. Why, that would be just... unthinkable. That would be admitting defeat. I've never admitted defeat on a computer problem, to my memory. Nor has my son. There is always a fix, sometimes not acceptable or too expensive, but always a fix.

Newer Service Technicians, and even some of my friends who come back to visit, have a problem with looking at the desktops of some of my customers. Their screens are a mess! Stuff all over the place. (Not that my screen at home is any better.) Some customers are almost anal compulsive in the metric-like precision of the placement of their icons. They have to be aligned in soldier-like precision. Others are like me, kind of in a galactic cloud kind of thing. The Graphic nebula has icons over there, the User Group nebula is over there, with all those Newsletter and Article-like icons in orbit around it, and over here is the Download nebula, etc. And scattered here and there are asteroid-like icons, just drifting in and out of the desktop, with a few comet-like icons that just surfaced from the Internet Milky Way this morning. Each desktop is different, and none is wrong. I have seen some people turn away in disgust at such a mess (to them). But each customer sees things in a different way and in a different light. I call this real computer diversity and enjoy seeing what makes a person tick. Real creative people enjoy living in this kind of world, picking and choosing at whatever comes to fancy in front of them. I find this fascinating.

Screen savers used to be a necessity for people who wanted to make sure their monitors didn't have phosphor burns. Apple's original 13-inch RGB monitor used to sell for a thousand dollars, and one had to protect that kind of investment. Since those days, the monitors have really improved and screen savers were more of an enjoyment than a real need. People have the weirdest desktops, and some of them can be embarrassing for the uninitiated casual passerby. Some that I've seen... but let's not get into that.

A major problem that many of our Mac customers have to surmount is that of creating and leaving many folders of stuff on the desktop. There are lots of crashing types of events that can cause those desktop folders to get irretrievably lost or damaged. A good portion of my service bench time is the alias'ing of those folders, and putting the folders back into the hard drive icon where they belong. I leave the alias's back on the desktop where the older folder were, to avoid customer confusion, and explain to them what I've done. Most of my customers will understand this. A few will even follow through on it. Most though, just do it again as a matter of convenience and habit. I admit that even I do it occasionally and have to clean up my 'Galactic Universe' of a desktop every few weeks or so.

Arlene the Good, Arlene the Pure, on the other hand, keeps her desktop nearly pristine pure. Now you have to remember that she was also the Assistant Manager of a Bank and has to have things 'just so.' I'm very lucky to have her around as she's the same way as a housekeeper. Everything is almost always clean, dusted and in it's place. My computer room is kind of like the back end of the Universe, where all the cosmic dust ends up. Anything computer-related ends up there, someplace. If I have to find something important, that's when a general cleanup of my computer room takes place. If my room looks neat, Arlene will generally ask me "...if I found what I was looking for." Yep!

Inside the Hard Drive is another matter for most folks. Some people are just pack rats, myself included. I have to force myself to throw things away. REALLY force myself. Over the years, as a User Group Leader and personal friend to almost all my members, I'm always thinking of what people can use. You have to remember that I was also the club Librarian in the older days and archived everything there too. So I kind of save things for others to use, should they ever need these things. My real weak point is in the graphic field. I save desktop scenes for every possible occasion and need. I have pictures that could be used for newsletter covers for every possible month or occasion. Want a picture of a three-legged rabbit with a purple bow? I could probably accommodate you. Same thing with fonts. My wife thinks I have an obsession with some of these things. I guess I do. Lately I've been culling back my hard drives from over 275,000 items, and I'm now down to a manageable 225,000 items or so. Hey, I'm a lot better than last week, right? And you thought YOU had a problem!

One thing that we don't do in our shop is nose around in people's stuff. God knows that I have enough stuff in my own drive to nose around in, and I don't have enough time to do that there, either. Your personal stuff is yours. I don't want to know what's in there. One time a picture was on the desktop, and after completing the repairs, I wanted to make sure the applications opened normally, which they sometimes won't do when you change Systems Folders and don't move the Preference files back into the new System Folder. I double-clicked on the picture and there was the customer and his wife in a very happy time. A VERY happy time! Oh boy, I closed that one up real fast and deleted the 'recent documents' items in the System Folder. Yep, THAT application worked alright! Try not to do that again. Every time I see that customer or his wife, I just picture 'happy times.' Needless to say, I hope you're picking up a few hints here and there as we take this walk together. If and when you decide to take and save some 'happy times' pictures, or even some pictures you may acquire from somewhere else, let me give you a hint. Create a new folder and call it some drab-sounding name, like 'Church maintenance records' or some such name that would never arouse a persons interest. Never, never name it xxx folder! That's like a magnet that says 'open me.' Not all service people have morals or integrity. And they are people after all. If I haven't said it before, I'll say it again. If it's highly personal stuff, it belongs on a CD, or a Zip, or a removable hard drive that's not accessible by others.

I've had many enjoyable moments while at the Service Bench and have had many enjoyable Service Technicians at my side over the years. I've had my share of 'shocking moments' when my fingers were where they shouldn't have been. I have also watched some of my compatriots with their 'shocking moments.' Dangerous times, but along with the others, I laughed my ass off and had to re-assemble that part of my butt many times. I helped train many people in my life and found the teacher part of it to be very gratifying and rewarding. Helping others has always been my major reward in life. I can't picture life without it.

CHAPTER 17

What Mac Men know about their women (who don't use Macs.)

They're soft.

Besides that, I bet you didn't know that the first six recognized computer programmers were all women. I even knew their names at one time. It seems that they were all mathematicians who were called in to program ENIAC in World War II, eligible men being called off to war at the time. Interesting trivia for those men who think they're God's gift to the computer world. I use that for the women who may be reading this book. For those same women, may I also say that for the last two Digital Camera and Graphics courses that I taught, eight out of every eleven students were women. Now that's cool. I also notice that it's women who take on the Newsletter Editor roles more and more in the User Groups. And do a great job at it. Form, Color and Composition are where it's at in designing a Newsletter. I think that women do a better job at it in general than a guy does. Hey, my wife tells me when my clothes don't match. Not so much as doesn't tell me, than laughs her ass off when I try to leave the house. "You're not going out like that, are you?" Well, I guess not. I've gotten better over the years.

In the beginning, it was rare to see women in User Group meetings. It was pretty much dominated by men until about ten years ago. Our Group had a woman President about 15 years ago, then had women on our Executive

Board. It was a matter of survival. What did we need to get more women in the meetings? Ask a guy? Right! We needed women on the Executive Board to answer these questions. We started asking them the right questions and the answers came. The meeting topics improved, like Genealogy, Graphics, men AND women games, quilting software, cooking software, word processor demos and Tax software, to name just a few. More women started coming to the meetings and the meetings improved in attendance, as well as variety. Today, we have a woman Newsletter Editor, a woman who does our printing and a goodly number of women on our Executive Board. Finally, women are taking their rightly place in the computer world, besides the men and not behind them. I'm very happy about that.

Some of the best Gamer's on the Internet are women. Great Shooter's on Role-playing games. Good reflexes. I've had some good women whip my butt in Unreal Tournaments. You never know if you're playing a man or a woman in some of these reality games. Some men take women's roles and figures for that slight hesitation it gives them when their opponents hesitate before shooting a woman. Bang, gotcha! Some women take men's roles on-line so they don't take any sexist remarks or hassles about being women. Some women, believe me, don't need or want your protection. They'll whip your butt any day and twice on Sunday! Women pilots today serve their country with honor and dignity. I'm just happy they're stepping up to the plate today and whacking them out of the park! Way to go, girl!

Back in my X-Ray days, I interviewed for four X-Ray Service people. One of my choices was a great looking girl, tops in her engineering class at RCA (a good NYC school at the time) who earned her way through school as a nude model. Hey, she needed the money, but she got almost all A's in a male-dominated Electrical Engineering class. I was going to use her as a Mammography Service Technician. Only problem was, there was no such thing as a Woman Service Technician in the whole X-Ray field at that time. She would have been the only one. Management turned me down. For years, men service technicians had to adjust the pressure and other things that went wrong on Mammography machines. Us, the guys with no boobs. With a woman tech, she could work with patients there, as well as with the women operators. I was a tad ahead of the time, I guess.

The local Sales Manager at Computer Factory was against me hiring a woman bench technician many years ago. Fortunately, Corporate sided with me on that one. I knew they needed minorities and pushed hard and won. It also helped that I trained her before she was hired, to dis-assemble a Mac Plus in the dark and replace the Analog/Power Supply Board and re-assemble the Mac. The proof of the pudding was to turn the lights on and turn on the Mac. If the screen lit up, you did it right. It took three or four days running before she could do that. I was the Jedi Master of 'in pitch black dark' component swap-ping of the Mac 128, 512 and Mac Plus CPU's. Corporate heard she could do that and they approved her. Ouch! Didn't make a friend of the Sales Manager there, but I got my way. Our store was constantly in the top 3 or 4 stores in the 62 store country in terms of service revenue, which was mostly Mac generated. All that, and with a smaller service department. They were trained to be fast. And they did NOT have to be all men! One of my prouder moments! She later left because of differences with that same Sales Manager and immediately got a job paying THREE times her service salary. Corporate was NOT happy to lose a minority. I was happy to pass off the responsibility for that loss to him. Ouch!

One woman that lost her job at Apple, took on a role and ran with it. She started her own company that does all the User Group breakfasts for Apple and Adobe trade shows and did a grand-slam job. Carmella is very well known in the Mac Trade and the User Groups. I really believe that women are taking over the leading positions in a number of User Groups today. Maybe not in the corporate culture that is Apple, but in many computer companies. That makes me happy.

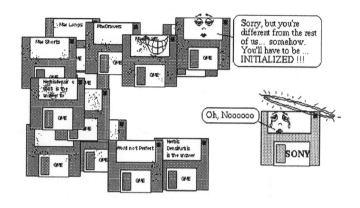

CHAPTER 18

She's a 'Mother' all right...

How can Apple survive after all these years of problems and now turning her back on her User Group children and loyal customers? Lately, Apple has been in the news more than the Iraq war. So many problems. So many untruths. So much unanswered. I've lost my faith in Apple as a company. Not as a platform, but as a company.

I've seen too many dealers and service shops getting screwed by Apple over the years. When it came to their AppleCare program, it was originally a great program. Then Apple started sending out renewal agreements around the dealers, and calling the customers direct for renewals, cutting out the dealers percentage of the service agreements. The dealers still had to service them, but wasn't getting the percentage of the agreements they needed for servicemen's salaries. Apple was using their AppleCare agreements as a customer database for service revenue. Then later, much later, that same database could be used when the Mother Ship opened her own Boutique Retail Sales stores. Now she was really pirating and plundering her own dealers customers. Holy Moley, Apple is now doing what the old Apple II User Group people were doing. Pirates! Wow!

Apple Dealers are now selling PC's to survive these times, and Apple is opening up more stores and competing with their own Dealers, taking their customers away from them. I see nothing but problems coming from this. Without that one-on-one local customer interface that people are used to seeing, Apple can't win this game. Retail is expensive and the Dealers' stores sell a diversity of products to survive. They survive by choosing the best of the products and marrying them to the individual customer. Apple sells boxes. Where will the users go to have things work? Today they only have the User Groups to fall back on. But Apple has been screwing them also. They get no support from Apple. Apple is using the User Groups as a Greenhouse nowadays. A place to sell their products with very little labor involved. However, what Apple is not seeing is that you have to nurture these buds to get productivity out of it. This is not happening, so even the User Groups are withering on the vine.

Apple's Research and Development groups come out with great products. However, some times they forget that it has to work consistently. Whatever happened to their great Quality Control and Human Interface department? Today, it sucks! Things don't work, they die, they take a long time to get fixed, then they break again. I'm in Service and I see this happen. Things started going downhill after the G3 Desktops and Towers. The iMacs had their Analog/Power Supply problems with $300 repairs and the eMacs had their same type problems with $450 repairs on a $900 machine, just out of warranty. Ouch! iMac's and eMacs with heavy problems, new G4's with leaf-blowing noisy power supplies and fans, new G5's with heavy power supply/fan noises, new OS X Panther problems destroying data on Firewire 800 external drives, FileVault problems, etc., and it goes on. How can it possibly be that no one in Quality Control foresaw these problems? No one tests vendor products with a new operating system? Not invented here–not tested here–mentality? Is there a Quality Control at Apple anymore? Or is it run by Marketing where a shipping date determines when a product goes out the door? I know it's just an opinion, but I think it's the latter. I have customers who have tried to get satisfaction on eMacs just barely out of warranty and have been turned down. Apple's reply is that AppleCare is there for that purpose. In other words, no AppleCare, no warranty. So sorry. You just paid $1,000 for a one year, two week old eMac. Sorry. I've had two customers this past week say to hell with Apple and go to Dell for a cheaper, more reliable (than their dead eMac) computer. I could not argue the point with them. Remember, I don't sell Apple computers. I never would have sold them an eMac to begin with. Too problematic (especially the early models). I would have chosen a more stable G4 tower system.

Now in the news, I read that Apple just did a number on our 'down-under' cousins. It appears that Australia's Apple dealers have just been skunked by Apple corporate. Their service contracts have just been side-stepped by Apple and given out to NCR, a private servicing outfit. Many Apple dealers, just like ours in this country, have been staying above water with their service revenues. Now that Apple has unjustly (as per our cousins) taken them away, what is there for the Apple dealers to do? I have seen Apple dealers in this country let their service people go and hire part-timers to come in now and then to do work. Stupid rationale, but the only way to survive today. They'll have to support the PC market as a side revenue, if not a main revenue. Either that, or give up on the Apple platform entirely and sell low-cost PC's like everybody else is doing and leave Apple to it's 'Boutiques.' Apple is in trouble and is wearing blinders.

On the Apple Software Developer side, they've all but given up on games for the Mac, and that's where the younger folks are. But 'HALO for the Mac' is now out, you might say. Yep; one ray of sunshine, that will only shine on Macs with a G4 or G5 processor running OS X 10.2.8 or higher. That's the minimum speed, folks. I don't see this a big seller right out of the box on the Mac side. I played it on the PC when it came out and really enjoyed it for a long time. I also played it on the Mac and it worked well, but not everybody in our group is running OS X. Probably less than half are. And our group has not been doing many game demos lately. Not for my lack of trying. It's just that the Executive Board doesn't think we should be expending our efforts there. Well, it appears that Apple has the same thoughts. They may pay lip service to gamers, but everyone they hire to run their efforts in that department quit soon after they get hired. Let's face it, Steve never did think games were the way to go. 'Think business machines!' I don't think Steve Jobs has changed his philosophy that much from the old days. Well, at least he doesn't call his employees 'worthless' anymore, as rumor has it he used to. We're in a politically-correct time today, as you may have noticed. Apple is after the money, as a corporate entity has a need to do, and is right to do so. For me it's a matter of how you go about it that makes things ethical and moral.

Apple has gone after the vendors sales for more short-term profit, with boxes like Final Cut Pro cutting out Adobe's Premiere, iMovie and others cutting out their vendors profits. Then Panther comes out with FontBook, an application with the same name and same concept as another OS 9 program, called, guess what, 'FontBook.' Kind of cuts into Suitcase and Font Reserve's sales a bit also. Apple has been doing this with other of their software developers. Another developer came out with an open Internet letter to Steve Jobs, asking him for at least a mention for Apple taking his software product, almost pixel for pixel and using it on Panther, with no revenue or mention of a thank you. Boy, even Blackbeard said thank you after taking everything you owned. Talk about chutzpah!

From everything I've seen so far, I see the big Developers like Adobe and others cutting Apple no more slack, since Apple shows no respect for them. I see Dealers cutting loose, along with their service support network. I see the Apple owners looking more and more at PC's as an alternative to the more expensive, more service-prone Apple computers. We have lost a number of our customers to Dell and Gateway because of Apple's service problems and the high costs of Apple parts for repair.

Apple has been shooting themselves so much in the foot lately that they need to hire more feet and a speed-loader for the pistol that they shoot themselves with. If this is a sign of the times, then I may be retiring at just the right time. I still love this platform and the people that are on it, but for Apple... she's a mean and greedy Mother!

As an old and almost retired Naked Serviceman sees it, Apple has a lot of work cut out for it on the Retail side. iPod sales are a short term thing. You can't base a company's existence on it. After they have their music and their friends music, etc., where do you go from there? End of sale. What takes the place of the iPod next year, or the year after that? Seeing as how Steve wrote the epitaph on System 9, there's no going back for those users unable or too stubborn to change. OS X has too many speed bumps in the road for heavy OS 9 users like me to upgrade all their software. Granted, those speed bumps will be smoothed out by the heavy OS X traffic generated on them and the patches and updates that'll eventually happen.

But for me, this upgrade path is too expensive to do both hardware AND software. End of sale. The gaming youth of today is learning on PC's, which Steve early on said NO to. Macs are for business, was the mantra. Sell for business. That message was like food to the PC shark industry. Programmers for games flocked to the PC side, which proliferated like a rabbit hutch. Early PC games really lacked good screen definition. Enter the video card industry for PC gamers. The quality and quantity of video cards made PC gamers the higher game industry standard. Today, if you want games, you look at PC's. Macs for games are second best, where you typically pay more for a Mac game than a PC game, and it's slower also. For games, it's megacycle versus megacycle. PC's win again. Damn!

Their prices are typically higher, and I don't see Apple changing much there, either. On some models you may get a break, but only when Apple deems it a corporate move. Retailers aren't allowed to set their own Apple retail price structure. They have to toe Apple's line. Too much inflexibility. In time, there may be no dealers to worry about.

At this time, I don't see Apple changing their retail model or their support model very much. It's worked for them in the past, so... Maybe Apple can be satisfied being just a niche player in the computer world, but I don't think so. Not with Steve Jobs at the helm. I also see no change in Apple's support of their User Groups in the near future. By support, I mean support like Guy Kawasaki used to provide. Pompoms and cheerleading and no bullshit to the loyal troops out there in the trenches of day-to-day computerdom. Geez, but I miss that guy. Kawasaki was like a breath of Spring air. His word was to be trusted. That's missing from Apple today.

CHAPTER 19

Problems Facing User Groups

Computer User Groups started by feeding on one another for information, software needs and support, which was nonexistent from the manufacturers. Over time, the User Groups thrived, since there was no other place to go. Today's User Groups that have survived, have done so by not relying on their parent manufacturers, like Dell or Apple for support. Our particular User Group has done well over the years by being self-reliant. As a Mac Service Technician, I've been very liberal with my support for User Group members, both in the shop and at the meetings. I'm sure this has also helped with our growth in the early years. Many of our User Group meetings had service strategies, like backing up and storage device techniques, as well as what diagnostics software they should buy. What was good and what was crap. What Apple models were excellent values and what they should stay away from. What? Heresy, you say? Come on now, folks. Those of you who think the IIvx, Performa 6100 and 7100 were models of Apple hardware excellence should have your heads examined. Someone had to tell the truth. I volunteered. Our members listened and prospered. They also didn't buy the Cube. If you listen to the Apple Marketing machine, you'll be buying everything off the production line, whether good or bad. User Group leaders, and their members, should provide that guiding light.

Now, with the proliferation of web site information on problematic models, one can be guided to those models with minimal problems. MacFixit, MacCentral and others lead the way in Mac reporting. With so many sites giving away information, the dependency of User Groups to members is waning. User Groups have to come up with more and more relevant topics to keep the members interest. If you can save your members money, you have a great topic for a meeting. Our November meeting is usually about Christmas shopping ideas and gifts for about $10 to $50 and from $50 to $100. What's a great value and where to get them from, including web addresses as necessary. Another great topic for a meeting is about magazine information. What Mac magazines are great values and great content? Marry the magazine to the individuals needs. Give examples of a magazine's content. 'Show and Tell' works great. Show them how to save money on subscriptions by using the 'bingo' cards. Waiting until the last month before your subscription expires for the lowest rates, etc. All the little tricks you can tell members about, works well for a meeting.

Having a 'Diagnostic Software' meeting night is a sure meeting getter. Getting some service people to show the members how to add their own RAM would be great. Even better would be a RAM-installing night for the members where hardware-oriented members would do it for them for a moderate User Group contribution, which would help the club treasury. This way, you wouldn't have to explain what a grounding wrist strap was.

Apple has not been helping with the success of it's User Groups, nor it's Dealers. If anything, the User Groups and Dealers may be a hindrance to the Mother Ship. The User Groups, with their feeding out of accurate and timely information may, at times, be disconcerting to Apple. Apple has, shall we say, swept timely information under the table at times, in order to further their sales, or in a hope that embarrassing stuff may never see the light of day. A good User Group will ensure that their membership will never be caught unawares, from any vendor! Apple's dealing with it's vendors, to this day in 2004, has been far from friendly. As long as you're not within reach of what it perceives to be a nearby sales opportunity, you'll be okay. They're even taking sales away from their own Dealers. And if they don't like it? Tough. That's the field they're playing in today. In many states, the sales tax is more than what the Dealers are making on Apple sales. That's pitiful. The Dealers would be better off putting their money back in the market for a better return. Their chances of success for a return in the market are about the same as it is for still being in the business as an Apple Dealer this time next year.

User Groups have to internalize. Think within the box of self-containment. They cannot rely on others to be there to help them out. Work on ways to get your own Projector for meetings. Use that Projector in innovative ways. Any way that a Group can project their self-image is great. Going to old-age homes and showing them slides of vacation places or pets or whatever is a wonderful use of a laptop and projector. It takes their minds off their own predicaments. Using the Groups' assets to further spread your image of a socially-conscious and community-serving group of computer people can only put you in good stead.

The media of today is unfortunately looking for topics of rage and misfortune to shock the headlines of today's newspapers and TV. User Groups can time their hopeful messages to TV stations and newspaper media representatives for a slow news day to get their news out.

I don't see the expansion of today's User Groups happening in any great numbers. Unfortunately for the Groups, the spreading of information is so available that large User Groups will be a dying breed. In it's place will be lots of small information-centric subgroups of amazing information. Very much like yesterdays and today's Special Interest Groups. Like little digital camera groups who use photo printers and maybe Photoshop or it's like. Groups of maybe four or at tops, maybe ten people who may get together once a month or so. Or maybe once every six months when something new comes out. I see this as a reality in the near future. Why go out in the cold when I can e-mail you immediately with an answer? Or, just do a web-camera group thing, where everybody can see everybody else and hear them also. All that today's User Group's can do to forestall this from happening soon, is to make their content highly enjoyable and more relevant, than what the User can find on the web at home. Leaders to make this happen are becoming rarer by the day. Leaders who can work together as a team are even more rare. I wish todays' User Group people the best of luck in searching them out and keeping them.

The field which once drew so many questers of knowledge has become so vast that the questers themselves have a hard time organizing themselves into groups with similar questions. It's so much easier today to just go on the web and search out your question. There are answers for almost every question you can think of. There are tutorials for almost every procedure in most major application. You just have to know where to look. You also have to know who to believe. It's best to really learn how to use a search engine and to use it well. You'll find that answer to your question. It's out there, somewhere. Along with every person you ever knew who's still alive or dead, every phone number and every address. Even social security numbers! It's just a matter of knowing where to look, or buying the information you want. It can all be found out there on the Internet.

My final thoughts on the User Group situation is that as a large social gathering group in quest of information, it has seen it's heyday. We have had our day in the sun. It has been a great party, but like all great parties, there is a time for us to quit and go home. In the morning, we can look back at what was, and with sadness in our eyes, hope that it can be again. It always hurts a little to look back and remember the good times and the good people. It would be wonderful to relive those times and give our friends one last hug. For old times sake.

CHAPTER 20

On Reflection

■■■ ■■■ ■■■ ■■■ ■■■ ■■■ ■■■

Since the earlier chapters, Apple has made some giant steps forward. Due to their successes with the iPod, Apple stock has climbed nearly to the moon and split. While I don't have an iPod, I can see the music-needy amongst you clamoring for the latest and greatest music tunes out there. For that need, Apple's iPod really fits the need. They have adapted the interface to where the rubber meets the road, so to speak. It works, and works nicely. Congratulations to the design team for a job well done.

An area where Apple may have been reading my mind is their prices. Just recently, they have come out with their Mac mini, which 'starts at just $499.00.' However, to bring it up to what I consider 'speed,' you'll need a keyboard, mouse and lots more RAM. Probably to the tune of $900.00 to $1,000.00. Don't get me wrong, it's a nice computer; small, compact, and has lots of goodies for the price. For the home, it's a nice second machine. For work or school, it fits nicely in a book bag or attaché case. Too nicely! Very easy to be stolen, if you get my drift. For somebody on the road doing presentations, it's a wonderful machine, especially for the input/output features of the mini. It'll see just about anything connected to it. Will it sell off the shelf, like the iPod? Only time will tell. But it appears that Apple is finally listening to the people out there. The price point is what sells computers. That's one reason the PC's are so successful and so outnumber the Apple Macintosh. People put up with Microsoft Windows over Mac OS X because it's so much cheaper to buy a PC. Once you try the Apple Operating System, you don't want to go back. But the price... oh my! So I offer my congratulations again to team Apple.

Now that I've been a cross-platform user (Macintosh and PC) for a number of years, what do I think of the differences between the two? At this point, in reflection, I can honestly say that I'm unbiased today. I like the way that the Macintosh can see almost anything you hook up to it, without special loading of drivers or software. It's so easy. PC's are about one to two software years behind Apple on that front. On the Operating Systems themselves, I'll also give Apple the edge. Hell with edge, they're a giant leap ahead. So far, to my understanding, there have been about 54 viruses for the Mac, and about 94,500 viruses for the PC's. Duh! So for safety, score one for the Mac Operating System, for now. But with OS X now being UNIX, who knows if that safety will stay a constant. Will the Hackers find the Mac OS a new challenge, or not? At this point, Windows is too easy to hack into; more so than the Mac OS.

Internet Explorer has been one of my biggest mental challenges. Pop-ups drive me nuts! I hate pop-ups! Those niggling dialog boxes that try to tell you that you've won something or other, or trying to get your credit card numbers. Annoying the heck out of people, while you're trying to do something productive. I recently switched over to Mozilla's Firefox just to get away from those pop-ups. Wow, Blessed Relief! No more pop-ups! I put it on my wife's machine. She loves the lack of pop-ups there also. It's now my recommendation of choice. Of course, on the Mac, you have Safari for OS X. No problems with pop-ups on Os X's Safari web browser. So, another point for Apple's software. Is there anything that I could consider negative on OS X?

Well now, you have to remember that I come from the old Apple school of software. The last great piece of software from Apple was OS 9.2. Very easy to back up, for Users and Service people alike. Very easy to find things in the OS. Bad System file; bad Finder file; bad Control Panel? Easy to fix! Just boot from another System Folder and go in and replace the offending System file that was giving you trouble. Back up your System Folder? Piece of cake; everything is right there. What you see, you can get; or copy; or back up. With OS X, it's now more like Windows. Half of the System stuff is invisible, that you really don't want to see anyway, since you wouldn't know what the hell to do with it. The naming convention of those invisible files wouldn't make sense to the uninitiated amongst us. We're not true believers in the occult of the software binary world. Therefore, you might as well keep them invisible, out of harms way.

For the casual everyday User, I much prefer the Apple OS X over the Windows XP software for numerous reasons. However, once a serious System level problem arises, I sincerely hope that you're backed up, in either System, because you're in trouble. The 'Help' phone lines, after the first couple of questions in either OS, will determine how deep they'll go into your System. Usually, they all follow a script, which you WILL follow along with them, like a bouncing ball. Lacking a resolution along those lines, prepare yourself for the worst. 'Format' your hard drive and re-install your software, using the original CD's that came with your system purchase. OUCH! So for System level problems, there is no winner here. They're both bad. One is a mammoth Windows XP half-hidden system, and the other is a mammoth OS X half-hidden system. Both require reinstalls.

Apple software, and lately, non-Apple software, is by and large instinctive and natural. Not so in the past. The software that comes with the Apple hardware is very instinctive and natural to the system. You can't say that with Windows software programs. Not all programs use the same keys for the same functions, as with Apple software.

However, for the mass market software, like games, you cannot beat the Windows side of the equation. That's where the sales dollars are.

Most games are for Windows machines. Note I didn't say that they were all quality games. There are lots of stinkers out there, my friends. Not all games are quality games. On the Mac side, for the fewer games there, most of them are quality games. Not so for the PC's. But the far greater number of games give the PC's the edge.

Graphics programs are another matter. In the old days, I'd say go with the Macintosh. However, in the past five years, the PC's and graphic cards, along with newer LCD Monitors have equaled out the graphics difference. I am an Adobe fan. I'll tell you that right out. I'm biased. With good reason, I believe. I think Adobe Photoshop, Illustrator and InDesign are some of the best, and most intuitive application programs out there in the marketplace today. These programs work equally well on either platform. I've used them on a Mac and on a PC. With equal RAM, I have no problem on either platform. Speed and ease-of-use is great on either. There are lots of other good graphics programs out there, like Painter and JASC, etc. But, none come close to Photoshop. Again, it may just be my opinion. I do teach digital camera classes and digital editing classes for beginners and average users alike, and recommend Photoshop Elements 3 for novice users and they like it and do not get lost with it. Ninety-five percent of my students use Windows XP machines. There's very little lost functionality between platforms and Adobe products.

For Office Productivity software, I'd say the same holds true. Give Microsoft their due, they clawed, kicked, scratched and bought out the competition, where necessary, and got their way to the top of the heap in this field. Microsoft Word, Excel, and PowerPoint have earned their staying power amongst both the Mac and PC platforms. While I personally think that there are better Word Processors out there today, like the old WordPerfect, I use 'Word' because of the portability of the files. Most everybody else uses 'Word,' so that's what I use, unfortunately. No winners and losers here; both platforms use the same software.

How about the hardware side? This is where the big difference lies. Here is where it's Apple versus the World. It's not Apple versus Windows, folks. Windows is only an Operating System. That's software. But in hardware, it's Apple versus everybody else. Everybody makes hardware systems. Even the guy around the corner can buy a box, put hardware into it, put a label "George's Computer Co." on it and sell it. Oh sure, he'll install Windows XP on it, or Linux, or whatever you want installed. So, it's definitely Apple versus everybody else. And everybody else can, and will do it, cheaper than Apple can. It's a numbers issue. Apple orders 1 million of a part, and everybody else orders 50 million of a similar, but different part. Who gets the part made cheaper? You want a part by Apple, it costs you lots (read gazillions) more than a similar 'Best Buy' or 'Staple' part. Parts for PC's are everywhere, catalogs of them. Parts for Apple's machines are from Apple only. And, Service Parts are almost non-existent for the end-user. Today's smaller iBooks, Powerbooks, and Mac-mini type machines have to be sent to Apple for an expensive $300 PLUS repair, while PC's can go to the corner PC Service shop for an inexpensive quickie $35 PLUS repair. So for the hardware repair side, PC's definitely have the edge, no question.

With Apple's 'Tower' machines (read Big Boxes, like PC's) you can now find and purchase replacement Hard Drives, CD Read/Write Drives, and DVD Read/Write Drives. They may not all work, but you can buy them. You have to be technically adept and well-read to purchase the RIGHT Drives that will work with your Apple Tower Mac. If you're not handy with tools, you'll also need some technical help to install the drives. The same goes with the PC's, by the way. However, it is definitely easier to format and install hard drives on the Mac than on a PC.

So for Hardware, I would give the PC platform the edge over Apple. They're cheaper to purchase, cheaper to service and cheaper to obtain quality software. I know that Apple Users will point out the software that Apple 'gives' you for free! But I point out that some people don't need or want that 'free' software. They have their own 'better' software that works for them. Or they're older retired people that may have no need to make their own epic movies, or listen to the latest Rap music with iTunes, or burning DVD's or CD's of music or pictures.

With my years of listening to Windows and Apple computer Users, I have a really big one to lay on Apple. Do you REALLY want to make a difference in the computer world? REALLY? Make an OS X Operating System for PC's! I know, I know, there was a challenge in the older Apple days to do it. I think the Apple/IBM teamwork was called 'Taligent,' or 'Pink.' But it never went anywhere. But maybe the timing wasn't right then. Now, the timing could work. Apple has the Operating System at a pretty good stage. It works okay, the interface looks great, and the User response is very positive. Right now, for my Windows XP Operating System, there are little 'hacks,' or add on utilities, that make Windows XP have some of the same characteristics of Apple's OS X. Little visual goodies like opaque folders and windows, whereby you can see what's underneath the current topmost window, or folder. I know it's just a little thing, by and of itself, but it is a visual 'gotcha.' Add another five or ten goodies, and you can have a desktop interface similar to the Apple Desktop interface. I've noticed lots of Windows people who think this is really nice. When I tell them that Apple does this in its Operating System, they have eyes wide and ask why Windows doesn't have it. I tell them "just wait a year or two." But what if they could buy the Operating System from Apple optimized for the PC right now?

Windows people would buy it off of the shelves. You couldn't make it fast enough. People are not that happy with Windows XP, as good as it is. What with the Viruses, the bugs, the massiveness of it, the cost and the constant need for Service Packs and updates; a new Apple look would be a breath of Spring for Windows Users. By keeping the price inline with Apple's OS X, it would therefore be cheaper than Windows XP.

There are Apple people who would think that it would be heresy to do this kind of thing. What would happen to the Apple hardware platform if this would happen? Well, think about it. If the Apple hardware was as superior as Apple Users say, it would still sell, wouldn't it? A Mercedes is a Mercedes is a Mercedes. They might not be able to get the same high prices they do today, but they'd still sell. Besides, Apple is not selling as many of their Tower Mac's as they once were. Their money today is from the iPod's, Laptops and miscellaneous markets, not from the Mac Towers. I think Twenty million sales of a PC version of OS X would definitely change Apple's mind. Then there's the 'newer and most-fantastic, golly-gee-whiz' version of OS X upgrades for the following year, etc. And also remember, what takes Microsoft three years to accomplish for a newer greater Operating System, only takes Apple One year! Oh yeah, there's lots of money in the sales and upgrades of Operating Systems. Ask Microsoft about that! Apple's hardware sales pales in the shadows of what they could do in the software field in the PC world.

Apple's Research and Development team is probably the best in the world for new thinking out of the box. Their designs are copied in everything from toasters to TV's, to new glassware colors. This is also a marketable product. Apple has a lot going for it, in many ways. But their blinders are still in place. Maybe the days of their outside-owned Retail stores are gone. Maybe they will eventually succeed with their own Retail stores where Gateway failed. But they still only have three percent or less of the computer hardware market total. I really believe that Apple has to totally change their concept of an Apple-only Operating System to achieve what Microsoft has accomplished. To expand out of their Apple-only closed universe, let the PC world get a taste of a really cool interface today, and not waiting for Microsoft for a year or two to catch up.

I've been down that old dusty road of marketing, sales and service; and have been a user on both Apple and PC platforms; and have also taught classes and led User Groups. Sometimes plain folks like us get tired of the daily hype and 'bullshit' from Marketing types and subliminal advertising. Apple's computers and PC's are getting so much alike today, that the average consumer would not have any difficulty in buying a PC with an Apple Operating System. It's not like the Early Daze, with the 'Them versus Us' philosophy. Today, I just want to get the job done, in the cheapest way I can. However, that's only one 'Old Guys' well-traveled opinion.

CHAPTER 21

Thanks for the journey

I have really appreciated your time in accompanying me through the journey of my life and times on the Service Bench and my times with the Macintosh platform. It was nice revisiting those times and places of years ago. I know that you can 'never go back' to those times again, but it almost felt that I was there as we were chatting it up during our walk.

There will be those who read this talk that we've had and will think it was a nasty thing for me to talk that way about 'the hand that feeds me.' For those detractors, may I remind you of one of my earlier maxims regarding Apple? "When starving with the tiger, the tiger starves last." Apple does not love me. Apple does not want to sleep with me. Apple does not care about me, one way or the other, except as a constant revenue stream. That's exactly what our Apple User Groups are to Apple. And we're very cheap. We're self-sustaining, cost them nothing and we excuse their weaknesses and absolve them of all guilt. Most of us.

I have paid my dues at the altar of Apple, and have genuflected and bowed in the early days along with the rest of you. But lately, especially in the past year or two, I find that my priestly robes have lost the glitter that they once had. I'm no longer the acolyte I used to be. I'm seeing that the icons of worship are made of plaster after all, and lately being fashioned and shaped by marketing types, and not the all-seeing visionaries that were there in the beginning. They had the vision of changing the world, one icon at a time. They did do that, but the world of today isn't the way it was then. Dreams are a wonderful thing. The Dreamers are even more wonderful.

Thank you again for sharing these memories with me. You've made them so real again for me.

George M. Engel
Lakeland, FL 33809
© copyright February 2004

"I claim full responsibility for the drawing of the old bit-map cartoons which were done in 1985's Mac 128 / Mac 512k's floppy disk era, using the drawing programs of the times. It kind of gives an old-time era feeling of the chapters in the book. Besides, it gives you an insight into the way my mind works. Now that's a scary vision in and of itself!" - GME

www.ingramcontent.com/pod-product-compliance
Lightning Source LLC
Chambersburg PA
CBHW051253050326
40689CB00007B/1182